T0077953

THE
DELIVERY
ROOM

KNOWING WHEN YOU ARE IN SPIRITUAL LABOR
AND WHEN TO CALL IN THE MIDWIVES

DAPHNE JETT

authorHOUSE·

AuthorHouse™
1663 Liberty Drive
Bloomington, IN 47403
www.authorhouse.com
Phone: 833-262-8899

Published by AuthorHouse 05/04/2022

ISBN: 978-1-6655-5824-2 (sc)
ISBN: 978-1-6655-5901-0 (e)

Print information available on the last page.

All verses are MEV unless otherwise noted.

This book is printed on acid-free paper.

CONTENTS

DEDICATION

I dedicate this book to Christ, the author and finisher. Thanks to the Holy Spirit for orchestrating my thoughts. To my husband, Kevin Jett, for being my support system throughout my life's journey. To my son, Kevin Jett Jr., you are my life's joy. To my mother, Geraldine Marie Barron, I will always love you. You have been one of my most prominent supporters. To you, God's sons and daughters, I have been assigned to author this book because of you.

INTRODUCTION

Let me start by saying thank You, Lord, for showing me who I am and why I am. I humbly accept and submit to the identity You have given me. Even though the process of being mended and molded was uncomfortable, You still comforted and loved me. Thank You for stripping away the identity I took on, based on the world's view of me. Thank You for rebuilding, repairing, reconditioning, and repositioning me.

Even when I had to die spiritually to myself, You resuscitated me secretly, without an audience. Thank You for the turbulence, the heartaches, the headaches, the uncomfortable encounters, and the trials I endured throughout my life's journey. It was in these moments that I drew near to You. Drawing closer to You caused me to know You more and pulled me into a place of intimacy with You. I am thankful that after many years of getting to know You and establishing an authentic relationship with you, I know Your Word to be accurate. I know Your Word to be true. I know Your Word to be You. I know You created all things. I trust you, God.

I surrender my life to Your will and Your way. You loved me unconditionally through the process of relinquishing my pain. Thank You for giving me purpose and a reason to live. Thank You for calling me. Thank You for stretching me beyond what I believed to be my capacity. Thank You for birthing something so much bigger than me. Thank You to the midwives You sent to coach and support me through carrying my purpose and spiritual travail. Thank You to the midwives and my support system for supporting me, even after I birthed my purpose. You ensured my safety, provided great counsel, and prepared me for the nurturing process. May Your purpose be fulfilled through my life. I am thankful.

As a child, I spent my summers with my aunt in the wild and wonderful land of West Virginia. Going to church was not an option in my aunt's home. We had to be at Sunday school, Sunday morning service, Sunday evening service, and midweek Bible study (and do not forget choir practice; however, choir practice was my choice). Each night before bed, my aunt, cousins, and I would form a big circle, and each of us had to pray aloud. There were no exceptions to the rule. As I reflect on these times, I remember our time in prayer, but I also remember sitting still in church, not saying one word to keep me from being scolded by my aunt or called out by the pastor. I can remember not being allowed to chew gum because it was considered disrespectful. If you were found guilty of chewing gum, the usher would bring you a tissue and tell you to spit it out.

I also recalled quietly putting one finger up to be excused from service to go to the restroom. There were specific clothing and accessories that associated you with holiness. I did not see where women were in the pulpit. Women were primarily seen in the choir, on the usher or nurse team, and standing at a podium on the floor giving the announcements. There were few sermons in church or conversations about purpose, your calling, or destiny. Still, there were plenty of stories throughout the Old Testament where people birthed their purpose and fulfilled God's plan.

Mary was spiritually impregnated with Jesus Christ through the Holy Spirit. The Holy Spirit impregnated Mary. Mary's purpose was to birth the Messiah, Jesus Christ. Wow, what an honor. How about Elizabeth, Mary's cousin? Elizabeth gave birth to John the Baptist, which was a miracle because she and her husband, Zechariah, thought she could not conceive a child because of their age. But God knew otherwise. Despite their old age, she became pregnant and birthed a son, John the Baptist, who was a great prophet whose purpose was to prepare the way for Jesus Christ. That, again, is purpose. People born with a purpose and calling have been a part of the Bible since God began to create, but this topic was not usually discussed in the church.

In recent years, however, purpose has been a hot topic in the pulpit, on social media, and at conference events. Everyone is speaking and teaching about purpose wherever you go. Can you say "surface"? Purpose is being solicited as nothing more than an empty shell, with no insight into what purpose means. Therefore, people are looking to find their purpose in an empty place. There is so much more to understanding your God-given purpose. I am not speaking of talents; that is another topic for another book. When teaching about walking in a God-ordained purpose, finding your calling, or fulfilling your destiny, you must lay the foundation of content, truth, and context about the journey. You do not just find your purpose. There are so many steps in discovering your purpose and birthing your purpose before walking into who God ordained you to be.

When there is no foundation laid about discovering your purpose, it leaves you wondering how to identify your purpose; you may wonder if you will ever identify it. If you tried to find your purpose and still have not discovered it, you may be left with a sense of failure. What does this mean? We must provide insight into the pursuit of purpose. In the journey of discovering your purpose, there are phases you must face in order to walk into who God has designed you to be. Jesus paid a hefty price as He completed His journey on earth. Jesus's sole purpose for coming to earth was to shed His precious blood on the cross to atone for our sins.

How can you walk in purpose, run into destiny, and fulfill the promise of God if you do not go through the process? Newsflash: The process must come before the promise. God does not just grant you the promise without taking you through a process of stripping and rebuilding. Think about the many stages that a mother faces when preparing to give birth to a child.

An expectant mother does not find out she is pregnant and then give birth to the baby. Nor does she give birth to the child when she discovers the baby's gender. There is a nine-month process she has to go through. The birth process goes from conception to the delivery room to give birth. It is the same when you go through understanding purpose. Before discovering your purpose, you must first establish an intimate relationship with God. You establish intimacy with God by developing a closer relationship with Him. It is the place where you find your true identity. You must get to know the Father first. In knowing Him, you are connected to the Holy Spirit and begin to learn who you are in Him. You have to first find your true identity in Christ and then accept that your purpose is in a dormant state until it is awakened or activated.

Throughout this book, you will gain insight from awakening your purpose to birthing your purpose. Depending on the size and weight of the purpose you carry, the stretching and the journey can take more time. You will learn more about the awakening of your purpose. There must be a time of preparation. Preparation is essential to ensure you can birth that which you carry. Preparation is not an overnight process. Preparing for the birth of your promise takes time. You must finish every stage of the process. I spent many years coaching, ministering, and counseling others, and in my experience, people struggle to find their purpose in life. People struggle because they look for their purpose based on what they want. They ask questions like, "What are my goals?" What are my aspirations? And what is it that I want out of life? People make their life's purpose about them by asking questions such as, "What are my dreams?"

God's purpose for your life is more significant than your fleshly assumptions or desires. God's purpose is to fulfill His plan on earth. It is not until you seek God's plan for your life that you find your true identity and purpose in Him. You must understand your "why." God is looking for authenticity. When it comes to an authentic relationship with Him, you must be ready to be reconstructed.

You find out your purpose, you must first come to know who you are in Christ. It is not about who people say you are. Knowing who you are originates in knowing who God is. When you understand how accepted and free, He has made you, you will become steadfast in your true self. You will change the world when you know who you are in Christ. Reading the Word and researching the scriptures helps you discover an intimate and authentic relationship with Him. It is not enough to know who others say Christ is or know of Him but knowing Him means having a genuine connection. It is not until you have accepted your identity and understand the freedom you receive through Christ that you become steadfast in your true self. To understand your why is to know that God's promises in Christ are yes. God's promises in Christ mean there are no limits or boundaries to your possibilities in Him. The sky is the limit. Do not conform to this world. This process will take you through a renewing stage.

You must learn to honor Christ in every aspect of our lives—in and outside the church. When you honor Him, you begin to identify with your purpose and are determined to fulfill it, knowing God gives you the strength and power to accomplish it. We must make Christ our priority by connecting with Him daily. Several times in the Bible, Jesus Christ separates Himself from His disciples and others in order to be alone with God. Luke 5:16 says, "He withdrew to the wilderness and prayed." Make sure you set aside time to spend with Christ. It is hard to have an authentic relationship with someone if you never spend time with them.

When it comes to having an authentic relationship with Christ, we must spend time getting to know Him. We must be intentional and purposeful when making time for God. Through His Word, God wants us to get to know Him more. God wants us to want to worship Him and be in His presence. Why? During these times, He will converse with you and reveal His revelation to you. He knows you better than you know yourself. Job 12:10 says, "In whose hand is the soul of every living thing and the breath of all mankind?" God directs the lives of His creatures; everyone's life is in His power."

God has a purpose for each of us, and it is much greater than our own personal fulfillment and desires. We must realize that to find the answer. We must seek God to understand His reason for putting us here on earth. If your starting point focuses on you, you will never discover your life's purpose. To know why you were born, you must first start with Christ. You were born for His plan to be fulfilled on earth. Jeremiah 1:5 states, "Before I formed you in the womb, I knew you; and before you were born, I sanctified you, and I ordained you a prophet to the nations."

Through my life's journey and discovering God's purpose and His ordained plan for my life, I learned there are various layers to finding my purpose and destiny. Your purpose and destiny are different because your purpose is why you are here. It is the key to life. There is no life without purpose. Purpose gives you direction and helps you pursue the very thing God has ordained you to be so destiny may become your reality. Let me set the record straight: Prior to meeting your destiny, you must first birth your purpose. There must be a birthing of purpose before you can fulfill your destiny and the plan of God.

The Delivery Room is a present-day book for everyone. This reading is for all who desire to identify with their God-ordained purpose. It gives vision to identifying your purpose, introducing you to your purpose, and providing structure for carrying your purpose to term and to a place of delivery. As I stated above, to meet your destiny, you must know who you are in Christ and become aware of your purpose. I say this because of the initial stages of understanding the call on your life. You are not born knowing your purpose or, for that matter, knowing that a purpose even exists. There must be an awakening where you are made aware that purpose is God's plan for your life. To achieve life's purpose, one must wish to want what God desires. There must also be a desire to fulfill the plan of God through what He has planted in us. There has to be some engagement, communication, and connection with Christ that draws you into some level of intimacy with Him. There are four key areas of intimacy that must occur before purpose begins to grow in you.

First and foremost, you have to recognize who you are in Him. You can only find your true identity in Christ. You cannot identify with a purpose until you acknowledge that purpose lies dormant in you. God planted the seed and knew you before you even left your mother's womb. Therefore, the purpose has laid dormant inside you until you chose to learn about Christ. In Him, you realize who you are and that purpose is a part of fulfilling His plan.

Next, you must introduce yourself to your purpose. This is the place of discovery and activation. The place of discovery is where you move purpose from a dormant place to a place of awakening. You can identify that your purpose is there but never move into discovery or activation. The introduction is where you begin to stimulate, activate, and discover your purpose. There must be a trigger point to activate your purpose. The good thing is that God planted purpose in us, so all we have to do is take the time to water our seed through reading, training, learning, and spending intimate time with God. You will begin to see your purpose grow and mature, expecting it to manifest at the appointed time.

Lastly, carry your purpose and then birth it. To birth your purpose, you must first accept it, nurture it, and ensure you get to the final birthing stage. There will be an appointed time. It is vital at this stage. God knows us best. We must seek after Him. God has the answer, and He will reveal it to you. Matthew 7:7–11 says, "Ask, and it will be given to you; seek, and you will find; knock, and it will be opened to you. For everyone who asks receives, and for Him who seeks finds, and for Him who knocks, it will be opened." When you carry a purpose, so many things change as you carry your purpose to term. At an appointed time during the carrying stage, the birth will take place.

God is strategic. He carefully planned for us to serve a particular purpose, so He carefully designed what seed each person would produce.

We have to be selfless when it comes to God's will for our lives and not allow worldly things to determine who we are. The Lord's will is good, and it is perfect. By reading *The Delivery Room*, you will learn about ways to work through obstacles that will arise. You will obtain tools and insight on preparing and recognizing when you are in a place of spiritual labor, when to call in the midwives, and when to head to the delivery room.

There will be points within the book where you will discover the pressure points and weights that may arise that make you want to give up. You will read about the different tools and stages during every trimester and phase of birthing your purpose.

The Delivery Room will assist in guiding you through every step of the process so when you come to the point of birthing your purpose, you will make it to the birthing place at the appointed time, birthing that which God foretold before the womb of your mother. *The Delivery Room* is for all who desire to identify with their God-ordained purpose and want to understand the journey of birthing what God has foretold. There is no secret about what happens in the delivery room. The delivery room is multifaceted; it is the labor room, the birthing room, and the recovery room. There are stages to birthing a purpose. To sum things up, the delivery room is the place in the hospital where prepping and positioning for birth take place.

This book describes spiritual labor, spiritual birthing, and the process of spiritual recovery after you birth your purpose. It uses scripture and provides insight into the signs from conception to the birthing place's delivery room and prepares you for birthing your gift at the appointed time. It will cause you to shift your thinking, activate forward movement, and help you take steps to birth your purpose and not mistake someone else's purpose as your own.

Our purpose is for God to get the glory out of our lives. You can identify your God-given purpose and walk in it. Look at it this way: God honors it. However, it is up to you to be in pursuit of it. Purpose has been lying hidden and undeveloped for too long. Now is the time to find your true identity through Christ, identify and awaken your purpose, carry your purpose, and birth what God has put inside you to fulfill His plan. Remember, His will is good, and it is perfect.

Prayer Is the Key: Faith Unlocks the Door

*Rejoice always, pray continually, and give thanks
in all circumstances, for this is God's will for
you in Christ Jesus. We should pray without
ceasing. —1 Thessalonians 5:16–18*

Before you read this book, I want to pray for you. There are things inside you that God wants to unleash. You have the world waiting on you, and I want you to see its manifestation this year. This journey begins with an intimate relationship with God. There should be a heartbeat in every person. Prayer should be the ingredient of every believer's life. It is when you pray that you win.

You become victorious when you pray. It causes you to become bold, brave, and fearless. You obtain intimacy with God. Prayer is the key, and faith unlocks the door. We must seek God in order to learn to hear His voice. God wants to talk to us. Jesus tells us in Matthew 6:7, "But when you pray, do not use vain repetitions, as the heathen do, for you think that you will be heard for your much speaking. Do not be like you, for your Father knows what things you have need of before you ask Him"

Your prayers should not be repetitive but purposeful, meaningful, and from the heart. God listens to all prayers. For your prayers to be accepted, you must align them with the Lord's will. Prayer also gives you the strength to avoid temptation.

Jesus counseled His disciples, "Watch and pray that you do not enter into temptation. The spirit is indeed willing, but the flesh is weak" (Matthew 26:41). Prayer can help you overcome the temptation to sin. The effectual, fervent prayers of the righteous accomplish much.

According to Luke 11:1–4, Jesus was giving instructions on how to pray. One day, Jesus was praying in a certain place. When he finished, one of his disciples said to him, "Lord, teach us to pray, just as John taught his disciples."

Jesus said, "When you pray, say, 'Our Father, who is in heaven, hallowed be your name. Your kingdom comes, and your will be done on earth as it is in heaven. Give us each day our daily bread. And forgive us our sins, for we also forgive everyone who is indebted to us. And lead us not into temptation but deliver us from evil.'"

Prayer Is the Key: My Prayer and Declaration for You

Therefore, I say to you, whatever things you ask for
when you pray, believe that you will receive them
and that you will have them. —Mark 11:24

I lift up every person reading this book to our Lord and Savior, Jesus Christ. I pray that it touches your heart and that it causes you to dig deep within yourself and develop an intimate relationship with Christ. My prayer is that you are honest with yourself about where you are, in this moment of your life, and that you are open to dealing with the issues of your heart.

As you read this book, my prayer is that you are ready to receive what is for you and are prepared to be a word messenger. May you understand who you are, and in your understanding, come to your true identity in Christ, and why you are here on earth.

Oh, how good it will feel. There is freedom in it. Breathe! I pray you will desire to fulfill your purpose. When you act out of obedience, it will glorify God. He will get the glory out of your obedience, your pursuit of Him, and the call on your life, causing heaven and earth to collide.

May the Lord speak to your heart and mind, until transformation happens. May He will drown out the noise, so you hear Him. And when you hear God, you will know that it is from Him. I pray it will be apparent to you that it is the voice of the Lord as you become a student of the Word. John 10:27 says, "My sheep hear my voice … and they follow me." You will follow Christ because His voice is clear to you. God will draw you nearer, so He can teach you His ways. I ask God to guard, guide, and protect you, as you go through the birthing process. While you are in pursuit of discovery and carrying out your purpose, may God comfort and keep you. Ask God for wisdom, and He will give it to you.

James 1:5 says, "If any of you lack wisdom, let him ask of God." May you have the knowledge and capacity to make good use of it, in Jesus's name. Through the pain, the suffering, the heartache, the pressing, and the pressure, I pray that God will be your focus point and that you will put on the full armor of God. As you make this journey, you will be like a willow tree on the windiest day; you will bend, but you will not break.

I pray you will understand that what God has put in you is not for you but for others. that you listen to the Holy Spirit for instructions on protecting what you carry from those who come to tear down, snatch, distort, and destroy what is meant to bring life to others. The process must come before the promise. I pray that you go into the dark places of your heart and relinquish your pain to God. Everything that has caused you to stagnate, you will pluck at the root.

As you read this book, I pray that every revelation concerning your life is lifted from each page and sets your life ablaze. May it become Rhema to your spirit. Let the reading of this book ignite a fire under you. Maybe it will cause you to want to know God more, and in knowing Him more, He will strip you of the old person you once knew. The dead things, the things of non-value, and the distorted and dysfunctional things of your past will be stripped and removed.

I pray that deliverance takes place where and when it is needed, and for God to bring a newness to your life. May He refresh, revive, restore, rejuvenate, redirect, and resuscitate you in the areas of your life that have no life. You can then breathe and hope again.

May your heart begin to desire what God desires. And may there be an awakening happening as you read and a craving to move forward in the things of God. As you move forward, start walking in what God called you to do, so rooms will enlarge and be made available to you. That destiny becomes your reality.

I declare and decree that no weapon formed against you will be successful.

Even if it is formed, it will not prosper. My prayer is that this book enriches your life and causes you to seek out your purpose, your destiny, and in your seeking, you find what you are in search of.

I declare and decree that this book is a new beginning.

It will transform your spirit and mind. God's light will overshadow every insecurity and bring light to every dark place. There will be no trace of your old mindset. Those things that are not of God will no longer have access to your mind.

I declare and decree that you understand your responsibility for what you carry inside you.

This journey will be an inside-out experience because this birth is not just for you. The journey is, but the birthing is not. Be a light to others, just like God is the light of life to us.

I declare and decree that this book will stir up the gifts inside you.

It will cause what is inside of you to leap; you will have a Mary-and-Elizabeth experience. You will be able to withstand the process's pain and pressure, and not give up, but rather stay on track.

I declare and decree that you will breathe again.

I pray there will be fresh oil. You shall come forth in this season. I pray that you will know what it means to walk in love, and the Holy Spirit will give you instructions on what to do next. My prayer is that you do not take your reason for being on earth lightly. This purpose comes with tremendous responsibility; it requires maturity.

My prayer is that you learn what maturity means to God, and you will continue to pray and be a student of His words. God will continue to shower you with grace and mercy as you obey Him. Do not be selfish with what you have birthed, but give it out to others, so they may begin to know God.

I pray you are not arrogant or judgmental but understand there is room for every gift under the sun. Recognize that God is calling you to a place of surrender. He desires your yes. God will guide you along the journey as your gift makes room for you.

I declare the glory and power of God over your life. In the name of Jesus. I declare that you will come out the victor and not the victim.

God will speak to you, and you will hear His voice as He speaks. He will say a word to you that will cause the delivery to spring forth and see the promise manifest right before your eyes. I pray that you know the goodness of God and have clear sight and laser focus as you pursue what God created you to do.

Lord, let this book carry Your anointing so it touches every person who reads it, and let the readers take every word, every process, and tell someone else about the goodness of God. I pray that it will draw them closer to Christ, that it will cause others to want to be in pursuit of Who Christ is and why they are here on earth.

I declare that this book will be more than just a read in your life. My prayer is for there to be a time of transformation, activation, and shift in your mindset. There will be a stripping off of the old things. I pray that you move forward, walk in boldness, and manifest what God has prophesied over you, so you can meet your destiny. In Jesus's name, Amen.

CHAPTER 1

---◆◇◆---

GOD MUST BE YOUR FIRST PRIORITY

> But seek first the kingdom of God and His
> righteousness, and all these things will be added to you.
> **—Matthew 6:33**

In your day-to-day life, you have a daily routine. You may cook, work, spend time with your spouse, check social media platforms, and watch television, amongst other routines. Have you ever asked yourself why you make these things a priority? Why did you make these things a part of your daily routine? Some of your daily routines are nonnegotiable. But other routines are a priority even though it is clear they are timewasters. I want you to think about where God fits into your list of priorities and daily routines. During many counseling sessions with believers, I discovered that people do not make God a part of their priority list. The Lord is not on their list of priorities.

In the same way, you find time to do the things you love to do, make sure you set aside time for God and make Him a part of your daily routine. You cannot wait until trouble finds you to make God an essential part of your life. God made you a necessary part of His plan when He gave His only Son. When you fit Christ into your life, you establish relationships with other people who belong to God. When you enjoy fellowship with one another, this helps you draw nearer to God.

> Your genuine identity is found only in Christ and in Him alone.
>
> ~ Daphne Jett

Spending time with God through reading and studying His Word and praying is key. The Lord has prepared everything. He has abundantly provided all things necessary for life and godliness (2 Peter 1:3. When you spend time in His presence, He blesses you with abundance. A relationship with God allows you to be pure, flourish, grow, and bear many spiritual fruits. Your relationship with God's Word brings life. Your connection to God's plan gives you a clear perspective of eternal inheritance because of your relationship to God's purpose, restoration, deliverance, holiness, and dominion. He pours godly and spiritual benefits into your life.

There is no relationship with God unless He is a constant priority in your life. I can remember when my priorities did not include Christ. I knew of Him; however, I had not yet established a relationship with Him. It was not until I surrendered my life to God that I realized I was walking in an identity that my past life experiences and people had given me. That is right. I wore a mask. I was a people-pleaser. When I came to know God intimately, I found my true identity. One of the things I did when I decided to commit to putting Christ first was to make prayer a part of my daily routine. I would pray to God, not asking for material things but for His guidance. Yes, I called on the Lord, and I began to go into a place of prayer, and I admitted to the Father that I needed help prioritizing my life so I could bring structure to make Him and His will for my life a priority.

We are currently living in a self-centered society. It is a "Look at me" world. People want to do whatever they want, whenever they want to do it, without restriction, boundaries, or consequences, unless and until there is a backlash. Once there is a backlash, the first-place people run to is God, the same God they did not make a priority in their lives. People also go to God's followers. These believers make God a priority. It is not enough to want God only when it is convenient for you. But Matthew 6:3 says, "But seek first His kingdom and His righteousness, and all these things will be given to you."

If you are going to get your life in order, you have to start with your priorities. Christ should be your first priority. He gave up His life for yours. Look at what gets the greatest attention in your life, and be honest with yourself. Perhaps it is your kids, your careers, or your marriage. It might be your position in society or your reputation. Whatever you deem most important will get the most of your time and attention. Did God make your priority list? If you allow temporary, less important things to dominate your life, you will never experience the fulfillment of all God offers us. The first foundational principle in this series is all about God's place in your life.

Your priorities steer you down a path in life. To put it another way, your priorities shape who you are and where you are heading. This concept is seen throughout the Bible. If you do not put God first, you will end up on a path that leads you further away from God's plan for your life. There are two scriptures I keep close to my heart when I think about why I should make God my top priority. The first scripture that comes to my mind is Matthew 6:24: "No one can serve two masters. Because he will either despise one and love the other, or he will hold onto one and despise the other. You cannot serve God and money." The second scripture that comes to mind is Matthew 22:37: "You shall love the Lord your God with all your heart, and with all your soul, and with all your mind."

God makes it abundantly clear in His scriptures that He must take precedence in your life. Your understanding of Who God is and what He has done in your life should shape everything else about you. He provides you with all you need in every other aspect of your existence. He makes you calm, keeps you safe, lets you understand, and gives you opportunities to achieve what He has planned for you. Make God a priority in your life by reading your Bible. Solicit the help of a small group or a mentor to keep you on track. Take time to pray. Do not get so preoccupied with less important matters that you forget to sit at Jesus's feet. He is entitled to the first spot on your priority list.

I was determined to make Him my priority before anything else. When I made God a priority, I began to share the innermost, sacred parts of my life. I needed Him to be my first priority. I had a hunger and thirst for my Savior, so I went to God to ask Him to help me put Him first because I desired to know Him more. I began scheduling time on my calendar for Him; this was the time I would devote to God. You must do that. You find time for other priorities. However, you never find the time to put Christ on the calendar. Try putting time for Him on the calendar at the beginning of the day. Begin your day with Christ, put Him first, and everything else should be added to your calendar after prioritizing your time with the Father.

God knows you better than you know yourself. Why? Because He designed you. He imbued you with meaning and created you to carry out His plan. He wants you to love others. You must love others, and you should make it your greatest priority. When you love others, and you make loving them a priority, not only is it pleasing to God, but what you believe is birthed from what you love. What you think becomes part of how you respond. Brian J. Dodd (Ph.D., University of Sheffield), a pastor, church planter, and seminary professor, said, "When you know the depth of your need for God, you must yield your heart; and when you are convinced that God's purpose is far superior to your preference, then you are ready to yield to God and to do God's will."

I did not realize how lost I was without Him. I know that not being intimately connected to Christ caused me to be out of alignment with finding my purpose. I am continuously in pursuit of walking intimately with God. When Jesus wanted to get away and spend time with God, He specified times and locations. To spend intimate time with His Father, Jesus would retreat and go to a quiet area to pray. Make sure you set aside time and a place to do so. You should set time aside to be with Him. It is difficult to become closer to God without making time for Him. Set a time and location aside to be dedicated to what you have built for Christ; you must do this to become consistent with developing this practice.

It is a life priority to cultivate a relationship with God. In my relationship with God, I experienced a stunning new level of intimacy. I realized I had been functioning with so little of the Lord, and now I can say, knowing Him more intimately, that He is a Father, friend, counselor, teacher, and Savior. My faith in Him leads me to believe that following God is never a waste of time but rather a blessing. The quest for God's presence is never useless when done by faith.

On the other hand, making Christ your first priority is critical if you want to find meaning. Proverbs 18:16 says, "A man's gift makes room for him and brings him before great men." I will ask you a question: How can you find your purpose if you do not know that He created it in you? Intimacy with Him is contagious. Jesus is the source of all you may want or desire. Consider all that is promised to us as believers. Consider the idea that the only goal is to obtain God's promises and maintain a relationship with Him. You will discover strength, joy, love, comfort, and peace in Him.

Psalm 27:4 says, "One thing I have asked of the Lord, which will I seek after, for me to dwell in the house of the Lord all the days of my life: to see the beauty of the Lord and to inquire in His temple." There is nothing quite like being able to gaze upon Jesus's beauty and reflect on who He is, allowing you to be in awe of Him.

Matthew 7:7 says, "Ask, and it will be given to you; seek, and you will find; knock, and it will be opened to you." You can tell that God is paying attention here. He is a compassionate God. In this passage, Jesus tells those who are listening to ask, seek, and knock, and that if they ask, He will give them what they seek. When you seek, you will find, and when you knock, God will open the correct doors for you. It was heard. The correct doors, not just any doors, will open for you. Matthew 7:7 is an open invitation to engage with a generous God Who wants and loves to hear His people's prayers. Setting aside time for prayer and engaging in it is an important aspect of creating a connection with God. You must begin by investing time in it. Why wouldn't you want to spend time with the Almighty? He has complete control over your genetic makeover, including your personality, purpose, abilities, gifts, appearance, and other physical characteristics.

God created you to fulfill His earthly plan and to glorify Himself via your life. As you get to know Him better, it is reassuring to realize His truth. You must learn to trust God because He truly understands your personality. He gave you life by seeking out your purpose for you to carry out His plan. As a result of your existence, God's plan has become a part of your plan. As a result, you are His handiwork; you must go about your Father's business. You must understand that God has chosen you for the life He has called you to live. As Christians, you are responsible for telling others about Christ's resurrection. You must describe how Christ has worked in your life and saved you. The discovery of your calling empowers you to advance in the kingdom, walk with purpose, and carry out God's plan for glory.

Your genuine identity is found only in Christ and in Him alone. You will find purpose when you understand who you are in Christ. When you uncover and awaken your mission and your desire to fulfill it, God will give you the power to do so. Please pay attention to me. Understanding His plan entails understanding where you fit into it. Only through Christ can you discover your true identity. Genesis 1:27 says, "So God created mankind in His own image. In the image of God, He created them; male and female, He created them." Living a Christian life requires knowing who you are in Christ. You become a spiritually new person once you discover a new life by having faith in God. To get the most out of a connection, you must first comprehend the type of relationship God is seeking and the circumstances of the partnership. You must also understand who you are building a relationship with. Your ideas and experiences are based on the importance of having a relationship with God. You are constantly discovering new things about God, such as how much He loves you and how much more you can love Him.

When I met my husband, he asked me on a date. We would talk on the phone for hours, getting to know each other before entering into a committed relationship. Even as a young girl, I knew the type of guy I was looking to date. He must be a gentleman and kind to his mom, amongst other things. It was not until we talked about our expectations of a committed relationship and clearly defined our expectations of each other that we decided to enter into a relationship. The same holds true for your connection with God. The cornerstone of Christianity and the foundation of spirituality is your relationship with God.

The Value of Knowing Christ

There is value in building a relationship with God. The importance of being closely connected with God is unique. It is almost overwhelming in its power. When you experience His sovereignty, you will know that this power is from Him. Your trust and faith in God are rewarded with serenity, love, courage, wisdom, and discernment as you develop your relationship with Him. Since God created you in His image and for His plan, He knows you better than you know yourself. Therefore, you learn about who He is and who you are in Him.

Your true identity comes from Him. We often pick up the identity of who people say we are, and this identity is hard to change. It is a false identity that comes from the weight of the world. However, you never take on the true identity that God gave you. To become closer to Christ, you must recognize that God created you and understands you best.

God created you with a purpose. The more intimate your relationship with God becomes, the more apparent it will become who you are in Him and your life's purpose. Understanding your true identity in Christ means you have been spiritually created as a new person. The Bible tells us that "if any man is in Christ, he is a new creature. Old things have passed away. Look, all things have become new" (2 Corinthians 5:17). Throughout the Bible, God will reveal who you are to you. Your identity in Christ speaks of you as a new creation. Your old self has left, and your new self emerges and lives in the power of God.

You are to live in Christlikeness, where you exemplify the spirit of Jesus Christ. You can read Galatians 20:20 or 2 Corinthians 3:16–18 to gain more insight into what the Bible says about your identity when you accept Christ. When you walk in the light of Him, you will hear His call and feel His love for you. Did you realize that Jesus's blood rescued you? He cares so much about you that He willingly gave His life for you. Why wouldn't you want an intimate relationship with Him, I wonder? It is the same thing with your mother and father. You recognize their voice when they discipline you or ask you to do something.

Do you remember when you were outside playing with your friends and your parents' only restriction was that you had to be inside before the streetlights turned on? You had to be home before dark. You knew it was not acceptable to be on the porch or in the driveway. Being home before the streetlights came on meant being in the house before dark. It did not matter where you were at the time; you knew two things: watch the time, the streetlights, and be in the house before dark. If you were not in the house by the time the streetlights came on, your parents would come outside and call you. You would hear the voice of your mother or your father calling you, and you would respond instantly because you know their voices.

Recognizing the voice of your parents is no different than knowing God's voice. When God calls, you should respond the same way you respond when your parents call your name. When you start a relationship with God, you create a closeness that makes you want Him more and more. Psalm 34:8 says, "Taste and see that the Lord is good; blessed is the man who takes refuge in Him." In Him, you live, move, and have your being.

Once you encounter God and have the opportunity to be in His presence, you will want to know more about Him. The more you learn about Him, the more you will understand Him. God is the beginning and the end. He is the beginning of everything and the conclusion. He created you to help others. You begin to witness the impact of getting to know Him better throughout the relationship-building stage. He will deal with heart purification, strongholds being shattered, chains being broken, and much more.

God will alter your course. When you get to know Him, He will change the atmosphere around you. If you begin to trust God with your secrets, you will find that He keeps them. You will not make it to the birthing room unless you first figure out Who He is and how He can help you birth your God-given mission. Accept yourself as you are in Him and recognize that you were created with a purpose. That is all there is to it. Later in the chapter, we will discuss the relationship between intimacy and purpose. When you connect with Him through the Holy Spirit, you begin to desire what He desires for your life. You feel God deserves your entire life and are willing to give it to Him. He is worthy of your undivided attention. To learn more, you must be willing to give up everything.

Philippians 3:7–8 says, "But what things were gain to me, I have counted these things to be a loss for the sake of Christ. Yes, certainly, I count everything as a loss for the excellence of the knowledge of Christ Jesus, my Lord, for whom I have forfeited the loss of all things and count them as rubbish that I may gain Christ." You have to realize the value and worth of the redemption, rescue, salvation, and deliverance you receive through Jesus Christ.

When Paul viewed the world in the light of God, he called it trash. However, you must understand the value of the call on your life. It is from this knowledge that the things of the world are compared to your knowledge and understanding of Christ. You must genuinely comprehend the value and significance of the redemption, salvation, and deliverance you receive through Jesus Christ. When Paul saw the world as rubbish, he saw it through the eyes of God. However, you must recognize the value I am placing on your life, which is the realization that the things of this world pale in contrast to your knowledge and comprehension of Christ. The word *light* means "life." Examining John 1:4: "In Him was life, and the life was the light of mankind. The light shines in the darkness, but the darkness has not overcome it." The only ones who will have eternal life are those who have faith in God. Life is the gift of God to Christ on this dying earth. Paul recognized what he had in Jesus Christ, and he thought everything else was a waste of time.

When I consider the goodness and power of knowing Who God is, I realize that no sin is worth hanging onto when compared to the magnitude and enormity of God's grace and strength. Christ died on the cross so that you could converse with him, learn about him, and choose to have an intimate relationship with him. There is nothing more valuable than your relationship with God. He made us; He made everything on earth according to His plans. There is no house, no car, no land, no person, no money, no possessions that could be considered more valuable than your relationship with Christ the King.

You must begin to consider your life in light of the salvation you received as a result of Christ's death. Knowing Jesus Christ is the most important thing you can do in this life. Nothing compares to God's goodness, grace, mercy, and covenant relationship.

Knowing God is extremely valuable. You must comprehend the significance of what you received as a result of Him. Knowing God gives you access to Him. God takes on the role of guide and defender for you. He lavishes grace on you and lavishes love on you. He provides you with a sense of security. Over and over, He forgives you for your mistakes. You must likewise forgive others, according to God.

You must recognize the value of what you received as a result of Christ. He gives you His favors and corrects you. He directs your ways, and God directs yours. You have joy because of Him, and you have salvation because of Him. God is in charge. He is, without a doubt, a sovereign God. He is almighty, all-powerful, and all-knowing, and knowing Him has value.

He created you. He breathed life into you and imbued you with purpose so you could carry out His plan on earth. That is why you must make Him your priority. Also, you have to understand the value of walking out the plan of God as it concerns your life. It is bigger than you. This plan is to give God the glory and to encourage people to embrace Who God is, so He can be glorified on earth as He is in heaven. There is a value, and it is your responsibility to understand the importance of what you received because of Him so you can tell others.

The first step in discovering your mission is to recognize your genuine identity in Christ. So, before you can give birth to a purpose, find a purpose, or even realize the scope of what you bear, you must first enter into a position of intimacy with Christ. It can be difficult to realize that what God wants you to birth is so much bigger and greater than your mind can comprehend, depending on where you are in your study of the Bible and your walk with God. This is due to a lack of understanding. Hosea 4:6 says, "My people are destroyed for lack of knowledge." Thank God. You can ask for wisdom, and He will give it to us. James 1:5 says, "If any of you lacks wisdom, let him ask of God, who gives to all men liberally and without criticism, and He will give it to them." Proverbs 4:7 says, "Wisdom is principal; therefore, get wisdom, and with all your getting, get understanding."

It is critical that you get wisdom and information, which you can achieve by praying, fasting, reading, or simply asking for it. He will make it happen. God knows what He has planned for you. If you are reading this book and wondering what your reason for living is, the first step is to cultivate a connection with God so He can offer you clarity. It is only when you know who you are in Christ that you can be certain of your calling. Make an effort to maintain a regular relationship with God. Relationships that lack engagement and consistency are doomed to fail. My hope is that God silences the background noise so you can hear the Lord and find Him in your search. It is energizing and enlightening to discover who you are in Christ. In all that He does, God is strategic. He gives you a mission for a reason.

Your journey is typically a culmination of what you have been through as a result of your parents' choices, as well as the choices you make as you come into your own. God's intentions for your life are well-thought-out. Your path is determined by your goals. Your trip provides you with the tools you need to carry out God's will. Your path will help you develop character and provide the perseverance you will need to finish what God has planned for you. Every day, God wants to live in and through you. You must develop a connection with God, live in love with the Father, and have daily discussions with Him. It all comes down to your relationship with the Father and your faith in Him. Before you can discover or birth your purpose, you must become intimate with God. In order for Him to receive glory and complete His plan, you must encounter Him and move forward in pursuing your purpose and accomplishing what He has placed you on earth to do.

A relationship with God cannot be merely a surface relationship. God wants authenticity. He wants the same kind of love you desire from Him. You must deepen your relationship with God, and the only way to do so is to gain a better grasp of His Word. You should not be afraid of your relationship with God. Spiritual intimacy aids in the development of partnerships. It is all about unity. Listening to what God has to say is the first step in developing a relationship with Him. As you read the Bible, God will communicate with you. As you pray, He will speak to you.

You can talk to God about the things that hurt you, the things you love, the things you miss, and the things that have to do with assisting in the construction of His Kingdom. You can also be emotionally truthful with Him. You do not have to be flawless. He will never leave you nor forsake you. You have to take the first steps. As you grow deeper into this intimate relationship, you will have to forgive yourself for things that have been done or said to you and others you have not forgiven yet. You are all aware that forgiveness is difficult. It is difficult to forgive someone who has hurt you. You must, however, forgive in order for God to forgive you. Guard your eye and ear gates. Do not allow the things you hear or see to become a part of you when you know they do not align with the Word of God. Also, be careful of what you are watching on TV, what you are listening to, and what entertains you.

Be cautious with social media and subliminal messages and things the enemy hides behind the scenes, and put on the armor of God every day, so you are prepared for the enemy's deceit. A relationship with God grows through spending time with Him. Spending time with God helps to develop a connection with Him. The fruit of the spirit is created through a close connection with God. A Father-child relationship is developed, and your day-to-day existence becomes more evident to you as you begin to become a reflection of God. According to the Bible, God is trustworthy. He is merciful, just, pure, and trustworthy. He is a God of grace and agape love. You learn more about God as you discover more about yourself. In many circumstances, when you are struggling or unsure of who you are in Christ, it reflects on your relationship with Him. You must learn about Him. You are sons and daughters of the Most High God. You are spiritually created to be an example and to reveal your qualities by being grounded in Him. It is through God's teaching that He leads you to everlasting truth. Through the perfect life of Christ, He guides you in the direction of obedience.

The Bible tells you that God is trustworthy. Not after you pay attention to everything else on your calendar. Not after you go through your emails and media feeds first thing in the morning. Not after you complete your to-do list. Not after you complete all your work obligations. You cannot if you do not have enough time and energy before bedtime. After all, you do not have time for God after your work, your marriage, social media, or whatever else you are using as an excuse. You must intentionally seek time with God daily and make Him a priority, just as Jesus commands in Matthew 6:33. Make the decision right now to put God first in your life. Commit to putting God first in your life. Admit that what you have been doing in the past is not working and that it is time to change your ways and put God first. Pray to God and admit you need His assistance in making Him a priority in your life. Ask God to help you in this area and give you the passion and desire to see your relationship grow in Christ. Make sure you start your day with the Word of God. Starting your day with God's Word helps you become a student of the Word. Starting your day off this way also helps you set your daily objectives and align your plans with God's plan.

Chapter Summary/Key Takeaways

Take time to reflect on where God ranks in your life. If He is not number one, you need to revisit what is taking His place. Having a healthy relationship with God is a priority. You will never discover who you are until you understand Who He is. He created you for something greater than yourself. He created you to recognize your purpose and walk in it so you can be a light to others as He was to you.

1. If God is not a top priority in your life, ask yourself why, and work to make Him a priority by removing all activities that do not add value.

2. Why wouldn't you want to know more about the God Who created you? Understanding Him enables you to recognize your true identity in Him.

3. Remember that as you grow in your relationship with God, your trust and faith will be rewarded with serenity, love, courage, wisdom, and discernment.

In the next chapter, you will learn what it means to be in an intimate place with God. Knowing about Christ is not enough to establish intimacy with Him. You must establish a deeper relationship with Him. He wants to talk to you. When you develop a close relationship with God, His voice becomes familiar to you. "My sheep listen to my voice; I know them, and they follow me," Jesus remarked (John 10:27). Those who hear God's voice are His own. Once you make God your number one priority, you will crave an intimate relationship with Him. You will want to learn more about Who created you and gave you purpose through the Holy Spirit.

CHAPTER 2

————◆◆◆————

AN INTIMATE PLACE WITH GOD

Trust in the Lord with all your heart and lean
not on your own understanding; in all your ways
acknowledge Him, and He will direct your paths.
—Proverbs 3:5–6

When you think of an intimate relationship, you usually think of a physical, emotional, or sexual relationship with someone you love, trust, and feel close to. In the world, intimacy is defined as a sexual relationship. When you hear someone talk about experiencing closeness with God, it can make you feel uneasy. You must first acknowledge that God is a spirit. Therefore, nothing relates to the world's definition of God's intimate relationship. When people hear about establishing intimacy with God, it can make them uncomfortable in their pursuit of God.

Entering into an intimate relationship with God indicates you understand having an abundant and plentiful life can only be found in God and not in people. When you obtain a personal relationship with God, you are never by yourself; you receive peace of mind, and you are an overcomer of your circumstances. It is a feeling of closeness, love, familiarity, and trust. Jesus had such an intimate relationship with God. He knew that at no time was He by Himself.

God wants you to desire intimacy with Him. He wants to hear from you. He wants you to want to be friends with Him. When you are in an intimate relationship with someone, you feel you can trust and love them. You desire to be close to them. It is a feeling of being connected and secure.

It is a longing to be in their presence. You choose to be around them. Being in an intimate relationship does not have to be with a girlfriend or a boyfriend. You can also have a personal relationship with a family member or dear friend, where you feel a sense of intimacy through closeness, familiarity, or privacy. You feel comfortable sharing your deepest, most inner secrets through conversation with them. You feel as though you can trust them.

Having a relationship with God connects you to Him. Connecting with God is where you learn His voice. Yes, you become familiar with the voice of God. You will have the ability to determine when God is speaking to you and when He is not. The Bible says, "My sheep hear My voice, and I know them, and they

> For to whom much is given, of him much shall be required. And from him to whom much was entrusted, much will be asked.
> ~ (Luke 12:48, MEV).

follow Me" (John 10:27). According to John 9, after Jesus healed a blind man, "He pointed out that only the voice of their particular shepherd could recognize." Those who refuse to listen to Jesus's witness indicate they are not part of His "flock" (John 10:1–6). In John 10:7–9, Jesus claimed that He was the only way to salvation, dividing everyone into two categories: saved and unsaved. Those who refuse to accept Christ are, by definition, members of Satan's enslaved gang (John 8:42–47).

Have you ever prayed to God for guidance on a difficult decision you needed to make? You wanted to ensure that you were making the best decision possible. However, when you received the answer, you wondered if you were hearing from God. Have you ever rebuked God for answering a prayer request because the response was not what you wanted to hear? I am sure your answer is yes. We have all been there. As your relationship with God grows more substantial, you will become more familiar with the sound of His voice. You do not have to wonder if it is God speaking to you or not.

We must belong to God to hear His voice. Jesus said, "My sheep listen to my voice; I know them, and they follow me" (John 10:27). Those who hear God's voice are His own, those whose grace has been rescued through trust in Jesus Christ. These sheep recognize and hear His voice because

He is their Shepherd. You must be His child if you are to recognize God's voice. You can listen to His voice when you spend time in Bible study and in peaceful contemplation of His Word. The more time you spend in close proximity to God and His Word, the easier it is to discern His voice and follow His guidance in your life.

Employees at a bank are taught to discover counterfeits by examining real money so closely that they can easily identify a fake. You should be so conversant with God's Word that you can tell when someone is speaking falsely to you. While God can talk to individuals today in various ways, He primarily communicates with them through His written Word. The Holy Spirit, your conscience, circumstances, and other people's exhortations can all be channeled through which God leads us. You might learn to distinguish God's voice by contrasting what you hear with the reality of scripture.

Uncovering Your True Identity in Christ

Throughout the Bible, we are told who we are. Finding your identity in Christ means you are not defined by others but by God. God created you in His image. Romans 6:6 says, "For you know that your old self was crucified with Him so that the body ruled by sin might be done away with, that you should no longer be slaves to sin." Embracing your true individuality in Christ can be a struggle, even for seasoned Christians.

Through speaking to friends and counseling others, I have learned that so many of you are bound with regrets, guilt, and shame; you bring along baggage. Not only are you carrying your own luggage, but you are also carrying the luggage of others. You never think that these things can keep you from moving forward or keep you from living in abundance. As a result, Christ comes so you may have life and have it more abundantly (John 10:10). So, I pose the question, how do you expect to know your purpose if you do not even understand who you are? It is something to think about.

People must stop allowing others to define who they are. Their views can be opinionated, based on their beliefs, biases, and insecurities. It does not matter what they think. The only thing that matters is how God sees you. You must begin to see yourself as Christ sees you. My question to you is, how do you see yourself? Is it based on worldly views? Is it based on the kind of car you drive? Is it based on the clothes you buy or where you live? Be honest with yourself. You must take how you see yourself and begin to align it with how God sees you. Throughout the Bible, scripture gives a clear picture of who you are in Christ. The Bible talks about your salvation through Christ and how you are created in God's image and likeness. It reveals rebellion through your fleshly desires and sinful personalities, far from Christ.

The Bible also talks about how you should live a purposeful life, and God gets the glory from it by rebuilding and repairing us. There is no secret to understanding your identity; it is defined throughout the Word of God. Your identity comes from how you live through Christ. Before I go further, let me set the record straight: Many people claim to know Christ; however, they only know of Christ. They know of Him because they have not spent the time needed to get to know Him.

Many of you say you have a relationship with Christ but have never spent intimate time with Him. It is important that you learn the difference. Relationships usually fail because people do not invest time in them. They are only looking at the person's surface, such as their looks, material possessions. However, there is a deeper, more intimate part of a person, like their character, their integrity, and whether their plans align with yours, to name a few. If you fail to spend time getting to know the person, you only know the shell of them.

When you take ownership of where you currently are in life and know that it is in accepting Jesus Christ that transformation happens, it is then that you should live in abundance. You should be walking in boldness and on fire for Jesus because of how far He has brought you. When you accept Christ as your Savior, you give up your old identity and become a new creation in Him. It is so important that you let go of the challenges you previously faced: the pain, shame, hurt, embarrassment, failures, and unforgiveness of others and yourself.

When you begin to live a Christlike life, you will see that bondage dismantled from your past situation. God gives you grace and mercy, and they both enable you to own the fact that you have been cleansed and to know that you are unrestricted in Christ. You are no longer a slave to your past. However, you can use your past as a witness and evidence of your freedom, God's agape love, and your deliverance through Jesus, so God gets the glory.

Spend time in prayer and Bible study. When you live in the abundance of Christ, He becomes the vanguard of everything you do and speak. Make sure you set aside time for fellowship (quiet time to hear from Him). Setting time aside for quiet time should be the foundation of your relationship with God. Reading your Bible, especially as a beginner, is not easy. Before I read, I pray and ask God to give me the revelation of His Word so I do not misunderstand what it says. It is not about knowing it all the first time. However, practice makes it better.

As you make this a consistent priority in your life, your relationship with God will grow. He will meet you with all your flaws and develop you as you seek after Him. There is so much to expect as you spend time in His presence. Getting to know the character and faithfulness of God so you can walk in your true identity with Christ happens when you spend time in the Word of God. Spending time in the Word of God is where you can stand solid in faith that you will find strength, joy, and hope.

You must meditate on God. When you meditate on God's Word, it purges your heart and then reconditions your heart with His words. You need to make God a part of your daily routine. As you read the Word of God, meditate, and reflect on the readings. Memorize scriptures that you can recite throughout the day so when the enemy throws darts at you, your spiritual armor will be able to withstand the hit. Walking in the way of God and not of the world is key to learning who you are in Him. You have to decide to let go of the world's way of life. You must get away from saying, "I am just a man," or "I am just a woman."

We are imperfect people. God is aware that we are imperfect people; however, we should aim for perfection in Him. The Bible tells you repeatedly that the world's way is a pathway to destruction. There must be a renewal in your mind from day to day so you can fight the lies of the world through God's truth. Make sure you are not comparing your life to others but to the Word of God alone. Honor God in every area of your life and being. You should always be in a place of seeking God with your whole heart and life. You should pray about the will of God for your life and the direction He wants you to go in. He orders your steps as you are obedient to the answer, He gives you. James 1:19 tells you that everyone should be quick to listen, slow to speak, and slow to become angry. When you pray, be slow to speak so you do not miss when God speaks to you through His Word and prayer.

Know that you do not have to walk through life alone. Your strength comes from God. When you know your God-given identity, it increases your faith and validates you. Therefore, God validates you; therefore, you no longer have to perform. At this point, you know God has equipped you, and you have faith in knowing that God has given you the strength to carry out His plan for your life. What do you accept in your thinking that steals or blurs your God-given identity? Ask yourself, "What is my God-given identity?" This is essential to know. Not knowing your God-given identity in Christ affects what you believe about yourself, and it influences how you live your life. There is power in understanding your identity. Yes, power. Knowing your God-given identity gives you self-esteem, awareness, and confidence. If you know who you are and Whose you are, it changes things. You are not talking about empty words on the surface. The way you see yourself will change if you understand what it means to be precious in His sight and fearfully and wonderfully made.

1 Corinthians 6:19 says, "The body is the temple." Reading this scripture should change how you take care of the body Christ has given you. You can afford to carry what people have said or done to you. You cannot afford to carry the shame of your past. Do you realize that your identity is based on how God views you? When you walk in your true identity given by God, there should be a level of enhanced faith and authentication. You should not have to wear a mask because the Bible says that when God calls people, He equips them to do what He called them to accomplish (Romans 8:30). You no longer have to worry about what people think or what you think about yourself.

Your faith and hope should be solely focused on the Word of God, not on you or what other people think. When you accept that everything is really about God, He will put you in a position to understand your purpose in Him. Say this over and over and over again: If you do not know who you are, and if you do not know Whose you are, it will be difficult to understand why God created you, not to mention, you will have a challenging time understanding your purpose. Why? Because your identity and your purpose go hand in hand. Without knowing your identity, your purpose sits dormant. Your identity is a part of your gifts, talents, upbringing, and more. These things are connected to your purpose. Knowing your God-given identity helps you better appreciate how they all fit together and their role in your purpose. So, what are you thinking about at this point? I hope you are asking God to shift your mindset so you may think differently, gain an understanding of your true identity, and ignore the opinions of others.

You have an identity as a believer in Christ, and that is becoming a new creation. Your old self has died, crucified with Christ, and your new self comes forth, living in God's power and likeness. Although it sounds easy to discover your identity in Christ, countless people in the Bible struggled. However, God still loved and used them. Look at Peter. Peter was called to walk with Christ as a disciple. He was not some rich guy who had it all together and was a perfect person. However, God did not choose him based on anything he had. For example, Peter was a fisherman and had no education when God called him.

When Peter began to walk with God, he began to mature in Christ because of the things he saw throughout their journey. However, Peter is known as a fisherman who catches fish, and he is now known as one who catches souls and brings them into the knowledge of Christ. Jesus and Peter had a close relationship. Remember when Peter witnessed Jesus walk on water? Through the Transfiguration, Jesus's complete divinity was revealed. Peter is a great example. Peter is a leader and a strong influencer, yet Peter struggled with his identity. Jesus tells him that he will deny Him three times before the rooster's crow, and Peter tells Jesus that he will never deny Him.

When Peter was identified as being with Jesus, he rebuked those claims and denied Jesus three times, as Jesus predicted he would do. Peter began to reflect on what Jesus had said to him, and he began to weep (Matthew 26:74–75). Although Peter wavered throughout the scriptures, he was committed to the call on his life, and its impact on God's people and Christianity was still strong. There are numerous people in the Bible who wrestled with their identity. God used them to accomplish His plan. In the same way, He uses you, despite your weaknesses or whether you can be true and consistent with your identity in Christ.

Finding Your Purpose through Intimacy

Finding your purpose is not always as easy as it sounds. Many people wonder, "How do I find my purpose? What does purpose even look like for me? Do I even have a purpose?" The answer to this last one is yes. You were born with a purpose and for a purpose to complete God's plan on earth. If you have life, if you have breath, then you have a purpose. However, finding your purpose is not always easy because you have to work to get to this point. Putting in the work is where most people lose sight. As easy as finding your purpose may seem for some people, it may not be as straightforward for others. Why? Because there are various steps; there are multiple things you have to go through. You have to be okay with going through a process. You have to own the fact that you have to invest. You must reach a point where you are willing to submit to His will.

When you identify with a purpose, remember that it is not about you. So many people get it confused. Your purpose is not about what you want to do; it is about what God put you on earth to do in order to carry out His plan. God knew you even before you were in your mother's womb, He planted a purpose in you, and He set you apart. That is, your purpose and journey have been designated and tailored for you to carry out God's plan and call on your life.

You have to go through a process once you acknowledge that there is a purpose lying dormant inside of you that must be activated and awakened. Once you discover your true purpose, once you are devoted to pursuing your purpose, once you have carried your purpose to term, at the appointed time, you will birth your purpose. Yes, you will see the manifestation of what you have been designed to do. However, be careful not to rush or allow someone else to cause you to birth your purpose before the appointed time because if you do, premature birth can cause problems.

Think about it. When you are born with a purpose inside of you, you do not say to yourself as a baby, "I will start walking with a purpose." Your purpose is dormant until something speaks to it at that stage in your life, until something happens that causes an awakening and charges you to go out and find what God has called you and put you here on earth to do. Finding your purpose is a desire and a hunger. It is your faith, and it is curiosity. It is the hope of being something more significant than where you see yourself today. It is the overwhelming feeling that once you walk in what God has designed you for, it will fulfill the voids you have and lead you to walk in wholeness and boldness with the ability to impact God's Kingdom.

Purpose starts with intimacy. Intimacy with the Father, the King of Kings and the Lord of Lords, and the great I Am, the only one, the Alpha and the Omega, the beginning and the ending. It begins with Him and ends with Him. Your purpose is so much bigger than what you think. Walking in your purpose is not for you. God has a strategic plan for every life that still has breath. I always say that nothing just happens by chance; God is all set up by it.

It is imperative to know that His will is good and perfect. Nothing happens in your life that does not pertain to your purpose and call. It is not until you have awakened to your purpose, identified your true identity in Christ, identified your purpose, discovered your purpose, and birthed your purpose at the appointed time, that you can walk out the plan of God for your life. However, you must start somewhere. I do not care how fast or how slow; I just move. The purpose of life is to be in pursuit of and to live in an intimate relationship with Christ. In the place of intimacy with God, you find a new identity. Intimacy is also where you discover that the seed of purpose is in a dormant state and needs to be awakened. It is vital in this state that you realize your purpose is there. There must be intimacy before conception.

Jeremiah 1:5 reflects on God's love for all His sons and daughters. When a mother is pregnant, she does not just know that she is pregnant. There has to be a discovery phase. It is not until she takes a test or goes to the doctor that she finds out she is pregnant and carrying that which God has purposed for her. Think about it. You do not get to choose your parents. If God chooses them for you, He chooses them based on your life's journey to carry out His plan. Mary carried a purpose when she carried Jesus. She did not have a choice. God planted the seed of purpose in Mary, and it was in her place of discovery that she realized she was carrying the Messiah Jesus to accomplish that which God sent Him to do. Imagine beginning pregnant with a great gift from God and carrying it for nine months.

God's purpose for Mary's life was nothing like what she had planned for her life. Her life took a detour from planning her marriage to preparing for Jesus in her womb. God chose Mary for this assignment. God is strategic. He could have used anyone, but He did not; He chose Mary because He knew she would be a willing and surrendered vessel. She was from the right family, in the right town, called Nazareth. Mary was engaged to Joseph from Bethlehem; she was a woman of character and a virgin. God had an appreciation for Mary, but He also prepared for the mission of Christ.

Did Mary ask the angel Gabriel, "Why me?" Gabriel told Mary this was a supernatural conception from the Holy Spirit, which meant the Holy Spirit would work within her, and the power of God would overshadow and hover over her. God chooses, develops, and prepares each of us in accordance with His plan, not ours. I know Mary had another plan for her life. However, God shifted the plan she had for herself and her husband-to-be.

Think about the story of Elizabeth, Mary's cousin. Mary was made aware that Elizabeth would have a child who would tell her about the coming Messiah, Jesus Christ, and that he was to be named John. Again, God shifted the trajectory of Elizabeth's life so His plan could be fulfilled on earth. Just like Mary, Elizabeth, and even Joseph, Mary's fiancé, God's purpose for your life was strategically planted before you were in your mother's womb. It does not matter how you plan your life; what matters is God's plan. His will for your life is perfect.

People come to me repeatedly and ask, how do I find out what my purpose is? The first question I ask them is, "Why do you want to know?" And there is always a pause. I ask this question because if you believe that your purpose and destiny are for you, it is time to reveal the truth. Your purpose or calling on this earth is to fulfill God's plan. Destiny is a place for the sovereign will of God. God's plan should always be your desire while seeking what He has birthed you to do on earth. To fulfill your destiny, you must make the right decisions and choices. We will talk more about the steps to discovering your purpose in Chapter 4.

We all long for unrestricted recognition, approval, and intimacy, so we must learn to develop intimacy with God. Intimacy is a place of trust, support, and feeling connected with someone you share your more profound thoughts and feelings. It is a place of love and endearment.

Intimacy originates from the Latin word *intimate*, which means "impress or make familiar," which comes from the Latin word *intimus*, meaning "inmost." Intimacy is closeness. It is a place of security, but also of seclusion and hiding. Who else is better to share your secrets with? Finding your purpose first starts with being intimate with God, not other people. James 4:8 says, "Draw near to God, and He will draw near to you. Cleanse your hands, sinners, and purify your hearts. You are double-minded."

Having intimacy with God is imperative to your search for purpose. Why? Because He knew you before the beginning. He knows the plans He has for you, as it states in Jeremiah 29:11.

In 2021, I spoke at a tent revival, and I talked about how the perfect love of God casts out fear. One of the questions I proposed to the congregation was, "Do you love God?" Some people answered yes, but many of them were silent, as though they did not know why I posed the question. I then asked a second time: do you love God? A few more people in the congregation said yes in a soft voice. If you love Him, why don't you chase after Him? Why don't you pursue Him and find Him? Because when you love someone or something, you go after it. It does not matter how much it costs or how far away it is; you pursue it, regardless of what you have to do. Desire it and want to be around it more. If you love God, why aren't you spending time with Him?

It is all too often that you chase after people and things that have no connection or link to your purpose or your journey. You look to people for validation when God should be the officiator of validation as it concerns your life. Why do you tell your truths and dreams to friends and acquaintances but not to the Father, who owns everything? You will not pray to the Father, Who knows your beginnings; He has the answer. His will for you is so much more than you can understand or comprehend. You should want to experience intimacy with Christ. You should want to know Him more. There should be a desire to know the One who created you. Think about it. People have a desire to know who they are, from a bloodline perspective. They take genealogy tests or provide samples of their DNA to find out where their family originated. Make this a desire to get to know Christ more intimately. He has your blueprint. He is the architect of your being. Why wouldn't you want to share your inner thoughts and feelings? It is with God that you are never alone. It is with Him that you will find peace.

Jesus had an intimate relationship with God. Psalm 34:8 says, "Taste and see that the Lord is good; blessed is the one who takes refuge in Him." If you spend time with Him reading your Bible and praying, you will establish an intimate relationship with Him. You will begin to learn His voice. Learn His character. God wants to talk to you. He wants to commune with you. The Lord loves you when you desire Him. However, He gives you a choice. Yes, He gives you an option to determine the type of relationship you want with Him. However, to identify with your purpose, you must seek Christ, and through intimacy, you develop a longing to be in a relationship with Him. Naturally, you long for authentic friendships where there is a sense of trust, and you do not have to fabricate stories of what you feel or who you are for fear of rejection from others.

Christ is a perfect God, and if you cannot be intimate with Him, you will definitely struggle to be close with imperfect people. Being intimate with Christ will show you how to experience intimacy in a relationship that is desirable. It is critical to put Christ at the center of your relationships. You must learn to put God first and make Him your first priority. You must allow Him to have the final say in your relationships and make Him your focus. Through him, you find out who you are, and your purpose is revealed by finding out who you are. Faith is the key to drawing near to God and having Him draw near to you. It is through your faith that Christ alone provides you access to him. When you believe everything He has promised, you will find your yes in Christ. Why? Because God is captivated by your faith, not your achievements or acts. Where faith is lacking, Christ is not pleased. And without faith, it is impossible to please him. When you draw near to God and believe that He exists, He will reward you when you diligently seek him. John 14:21 says, "Whoever has my commands and keeps them is the one who loves me. My Father will love the one who loves me, and I too will love them and show myself to them." When you trust Christ and His promises and live by them, God comes and supports you. He will also manifest himself in you. People's experiences of intimacy with God vary because He tailors His response to fit the uniqueness of each person.

You must continue to be in pursuit of God. You should continue to pursue God, and in doing this, you not only find out more about Him, but you also find out a lot about yourself, so you begin to walk in your purpose. There are many ways to commune with Him. When you invite God in, you begin to build a relationship with Him. Any moment can build a relationship with Him. When you encounter God's presence, His presence becomes more defined in your life. Growing in your knowledge of God has no bounds. He is endless and immeasurable. There is always more to Christ, and you can never know all there is to know about him. This drive to continue growing your intimacy with God is the plug to becoming shatterproof. You are wired to seek an enhanced relationship with Him. If you do not have it, you are depleted, empty, and hungry for Him. However, with it, you begin to be the light that shines and displays the love of God.

Chapter Summary/Key Takeaways

Understanding the importance of having an intimate relationship with God is essential to defining your purpose. You have taken the time to get to know more about Him, to learn His voice so you can commune with Him and begin the process of discovery.

1. A close relationship with Christ allows you to recognize His voice.
2. God's intimacy teaches you about your true identity in Him.
3. A close relationship with God connects you to the Holy Spirit.

The next chapter provides an overview of how to connect to the source of it all, the Holy Spirit. The Holy Spirit will teach you and guide you concerning the things of God. Knowing Christ is an inward-outward experience, not an outward-inward experience. Once you commit to a personal relationship with Him, you will understand why He created you.

Prayer Is the Key: Acceptance of the Holy Spirit

Dear Father God, I desire You. I want to be in an intimate place with You, God. Lord, I crave to be an instrument for the Kingdom of God.

Because I am a believer, I make an appeal to receive the Holy Spirit, which You promised me. Father God, I ask that You baptize me in the Holy Spirit so Your power will arrest me, that it transforms me and causes me to walk out the will of God, fulfilling Your plan and purpose in my life so You get all the glory. I want Your Holy Spirit to work through me, not just a portion of me, God, but all of me, every part of my being, so Your Kingdom may come and Your will be done on earth as it is in heaven. Lord, let the power of the Holy Spirit take over my life. I thank You, Lord, for such a priceless gift, and I give thanks for being able to connect with the Holy Spirit, Who brings me into the understanding and acceptance of the spirit of God. Baptize me, Lord. Baptize me in the Holy Spirit so the power will capture me. Holy Spirit, grant me dominion, power, and authority to gleam in the spirit. The gift of the Holy Spirit is a gift I will not take for granted. Lord, I ask that You give me an illustration that signifies I have been baptized in the Holy Spirit. Lord, I will forever be grateful and give You the honor. I will forever be humble and give You glory, praise, and thanks. I declare it to be so, in Jesus's name, amen.

CHAPTER 3

SPIRITUAL CONCEPTION

Before I formed you in the womb, I knew you;
and before you were born, I sanctified you, and
I ordained you a prophet to the nations.
—**Jeremiah 1:5**

There must be a beginning before there is an ending. You read about developing a personal relationship with God. You realize how important it is to recognize His voice and listen to him so he can speak to you. Are you reading this book to figure out how to find your purpose? If so, I suggest you start with intimacy with God. The more you are obedient to the voice of God, the more clarity you have, and the closer you are to identifying who you are without the influence of people or things that cause you pain. And the closer you get to the call in your life, the better. You all have a purpose. However, not everyone knows their God-given purpose. When you are born, your purpose is dormant until it is awakened. Awakening is a component of conception. Conception is the start of something. Conception is also the beginning of new life in the womb and the enlargement of the heart of purpose, desire, and thought.

Keep in mind that anything you expect to give birth to must go through the process. Jeremiah 1:5 says, "Before I formed you in the womb, I knew you, and before you were born, I sanctified you, and I ordained you a prophet to the nations." When God speaks to Jeremiah, God insinuates that there is a time of spiritual conception, "beginning or planning," that takes place before spiritual pregnancy. There has to be impartation and then preparation for the release of God.

Chapter 1 discussed being in an intimate relationship with God and how important it is to establish closeness to Him. You must understand how vital it is to know Him. Each chapter will be a reminder of why connecting to Him is important. Knowing God is not enough. When you spend time with Him, you discover His character and His voice. Knowing His name is not enough.

When I was in high school, I was extremely popular, and there were times when my friends would ask me whether or not I knew a specific person, and I would say, "No, I do not know them. "My friend would say, "They told me they knew you." However, they did not know me. They knew of me. They only knew of me because I was well-liked. I had no connection with them, nor had we developed a relationship. They were familiar with who they thought I was or believed I was. It is the same situation when it comes to Christ. People are familiar with His name and the scriptures that they have heard for years. However, not everyone invests the time in getting to know Him for themselves.

> Make peace with the process!
> ~ Unknown

The Key Is Knowing Christ for Yourself

Knowing Christ is an inward-outward experience, not an outward-inward experience. It is not until you commit to a personal relationship with Him that you will understand why He created you. It is not until you find your true identity through an authentic relationship with God that you find your purpose. Finding your purpose has a lot to do with knowing who you are. Once you find your true identity in Christ, the Holy Spirit's power connects you to your purpose.

It is hard to find your purpose through the mask you wear every day. Why? If you try to identify your calling while you have a distorted view of yourself, you will miss the mark. It can cause you to be out of alignment with God's plan. I know you have seen this before; someone may be on the usher board who should be a minister, someone in the choir should be on the usher board, the person who should be ministering is a greeter, and so many other examples. These things happen because many people are out of alignment and have not established their relationship with the Spirit of God.

Connecting Conception

Let me be clear, there could be conception and no pregnancy. For conception to take place, conception has to be connected to a source. There could be conception but no pregnancy. Conception happens whenever a sperm and egg join together. When a woman ovulates, her ovaries release an egg. Once an egg is released, it stays in the fallopian tube, the part of the reproductive tract that connects the ovaries to the uterus. If sperm and an egg meet in the fallopian tube, conception is likely. If they do not connect, the sperm and egg do not attach to the fallopian tube, and pregnancy does not happen (Burch, "Conception: Timeline, Process, Signs, and Preparation.").

Anything that has a beginning begins with a seed. Conception must attach or unite with the appropriate source to come forth and be birthed. If you turn on a lamp for light, and it is not plugged into the right source, it will not produce light. It is not until it connects to an energy source, like an outlet, that it obtains the supply that it needs to produce light. It must connect to the source that it needs to activate what it was created to do. Connecting to the source, which is the Holy Spirit, is the same for our purpose. God wants us to have a new life, and connecting to the Spirit of God is where new life begins. I reiterate that there must be a connection. And once there is a connection, the process of conception begins. If you are not connecting with God, you will not understand who you are or know your purpose.

Being pregnant with a purpose does not begin until conception happens. Conception and eventually pregnancy can encompass a surprisingly obscure series of steps. Everything must fall into place for a pregnancy to be carried to term; this will be discussed in Chapter 6. Conception is a critical process, and potential complications could affect pregnancy at each stage. Conception does not always mean that a pregnancy will occur and be carried to full term. Let us discuss conception further. Conception starts with a seed. The seed is purpose. It was the Holy Spirit who imparted the seed of purpose (Matthew 1:18–22). Parents who go to childbirth classes learn the skills they need and understand what they should expect during pregnancy and labor.

However, there is never a discussion about the spiritual side of birth. Women who give birth to a baby are given a great opportunity to awaken their spirituality. It is the same with spiritual conception as it relates to your God-given purpose. Intimacy comes before conception as it pertains to natural and spiritual birth. Just as giving birth to a baby provides the mother with an opportunity to awaken her spiritual gift, when it comes to birthing your purpose, it does not just happen. There is a process to awaken your purpose. God gives you a purpose to fulfill His plan, so you are born with a purpose. However, you are not born knowing your purpose, as it has to be discovered. Your purpose is dormant until you are connected to the Spirit of God. Then the Holy Spirit speaks to your spirit using people, places, or things. You still have not yet reached the awakening stage. However, once you are connected, you have come to a place of acknowledging that you have a purpose, and even though you do not know what it is, you now know your purpose is there. So let us spot-check before moving forward.

When you develop intimacy with Christ, He reveals Himself to you, and then He reveals your true identity in Him. The more consistent you are in knowing Him and knowing who you are in Christ, the more you go into a place of conception through connecting to the Holy Spirit. You must acknowledge that you have a purpose in you that needs to be awakened to fulfill God's plan.

After you recognize you have a purpose inside of you, you have to decide whether you will seek to understand your purpose or continue staying in a dormant state. I have seen people go either way. However, once you discover that you have a purpose and begin to feed it with the Word of God, with words of affirmation, and with coming into a knowing of who you are, your faith begins to breathe new life into your purpose. It is like a person whose heart has stopped beating and needs to be resuscitated. It can take one or many attempts before a person is revived. When you first acknowledge that you have a purpose, it is still important to know who you are. You will never find your God-given purpose until it finds you. You are what God created. Not the masked-up you, not the fake you, the excuse you, or you that people define. I am referring to the you God created in order for His plan on this earth to be fulfilled and for Him to be glorified.

There must be activation that connects through having faith and the trust you put in God as you connect to Him and build a close relationship with Him and as the Holy Spirit speaks to you and reveals Himself to you and your true identity in Christ. If you turn on a lamp without plugging it in, you will not receive the supply of energy you need for the lamp to produce light. You must connect the lamp to the proper source to produce what it is purposed to do, and it is the same for you. What sources do you need to connect with to acknowledge and awaken your calling? It will take the Holy Spirit, faith, trust, and truth, and this will expand what is inside of you, nothing else. You must not look for purpose in people if God has not confirmed or revealed it to you.

Connecting to a Source: Holy Spirit

It is the Holy Spirit Who connects us to Christ. The Holy Spirit is God. The Holy Spirit is not a separate person from God. When you come into an intimate relationship with God, God's presence, known as the Holy Spirit, begins to connect and speak to you. The Holy Spirit also connects with someone to deliver a revelation to you or sometimes talk directly to you. Look at Mary, who was impregnated through the power of the Holy Spirit to carry the Messiah. God gave specific reasons for choosing Mary of Nazareth, and she was well respected by God. Her purpose was to bring the Messiah to term and birth Him at the appointed time. That was her purpose.

The birth had to occur so God's plan might be accomplished on earth. How about Elizabeth and Zechariah, aged, never thinking they would carry a child? However, Elizabeth became pregnant with John the Baptist. Elizabeth's assignment had a purpose. Elizabeth's purpose was to carry John the Baptist to term because His purpose as a prophet was to prepare the people for the coming of the Messiah. John would tell people to repent, as the Kingdom of heaven was near. This was his purpose. Make no mistake, you all have a purpose and what has been planted in us is priceless and precious. You are conceived through the Spirit of God. You have the favor of God in your life. He knows the plan. Jeremiah 29:11 says, "For I know the plans that I have for you, says the Lord, plans for peace and not for evil, to give you a future and a hope."

God's Word in Jeremiah 1:5 reveals that when God forms someone, it is a plan He developed before He formed the person in the mother's womb. God not only has a deliberate strategy for how He will create you, but He also knows you before you were created. When God created you, He knew exactly who He was making and the purpose you would fulfill once you were born. God is the supreme ruler of your life and behavior, traits, qualities, gifts, talents, and entire being.

God formed you before the conception of your mother and father. He created you according to His plan so you would glorify Him. God knows all about you. He knew your name before your parents named you, and He spoke it so you could be born at the right time to carry out His plan for the earth. As a young girl, I could remember feeling different and seeing through people and things others did not think I had seen or heard. I can remember being in church and hearing people speak in tongues and understanding what they were saying. I remember thinking and even questioning what was wrong with me, knowing that I was different, but I did not know why.

One thing I knew was that God had His hands on me. He would speak to me. At the age of fourteen, He anointed my voice in a small church in Montgomery, West Virginia, before I even thought about singing in a choir. I remember the day as though it was yesterday. When I began to use my voice to sing songs of worship and praise, the enemy would fight me. This was when I started reading my Bible, I learned more about Christ and the Holy Spirit. At the most challenging times in my life, I had to trust Him. I knew at the time, in His timing, at the appointed time, I would birth something that would bring people into knowing Him, and here I am, one of the many assignments God has given me. That was always my heart's desire to do the will of God.

God determines your path, and it is not always easy. However, if you connect to God, you begin to tap into your source and supply. Christ is your source and supply. Christ supplies all you need. He leaves nothing undone. God is the all-knowing, all-powerful Creator; even your difficulties were part of His plan. God was setting you up for something greater than yourself.

This is why you should draw closer to Him. You can do nothing without Him. The good and the bad are part of His plan. The Holy Spirit is the source that keeps us connected to Christ. Once you are connected, you will begin to obtain downloads. These downloads will reveal who you are and expose the why in your life. However, you must be consistent and communicate with God. As you continue to seek, the Word of God says you shall find. As you knock, the doors will be opened. As it pertains to conception, the Holy Spirit speaks a word, and once you absorb it, it begins to give life.

The Holy Spirit is the source and supply of what you need to connect intimately with Christ. Once you become connected to the Holy Spirit and continue to seek after the Father, keep in mind that when you open yourself up to the Spirit of God, your purpose has moved into an awakening state and is activated at the point you connect with God through the Holy Spirit. You are connected to God by the Holy Spirit. The Holy Spirit connects heaven and earth. Without the Holy Spirit, you will not know what you are supposed to do because the Holy Spirit is your guide. God gave us the Holy Spirit so we might know Him and understand Who He is. You can look at the Holy Spirit as your consoler, encourager, and helper. As you seek to birth your purpose, you must have the Holy Spirit as your guide. Without the Holy Spirit, you will never enter the doors of the delivery room. He is your guide.

Symptoms of Conception

There is a level of discernment when you come to connect with the Holy Spirit. The Holy Spirit will give you warnings and information that you would not understand without the Spirit of Knowledge. Know that you are connected to the Holy Spirit. Your purpose is in the conception phase, which marks the first step toward pregnancy. Once the process of conception begins, there are symptoms, signs, and upset patterns that take place once you have moved to conception.

As you seek to awaken your purpose, you must continue to stay in relationship with God and keep the Holy Spirit as your source and guide. At this stage, not staying connected to your source could cause you to miscarry and fail to achieve the intended purpose because you fail to stay connected and consistent in your relationship with God. When a woman becomes pregnant, there must first be some level of intimacy before conception happens. A woman does not know she is pregnant until she begins to experience changes in her body or experiences uncommon symptoms such as nausea, fatigue, vomiting, or morning sickness. It is not until she takes a pregnancy test or goes to the doctor that she finds out she is pregnant with a child.

You will know your purpose has been awakened when you begin to experience symptoms that are out of the norm. You will experience changes and discomfort that make you feel unfamiliar symptoms, signs, and indicators. You desire to know more about Who God is, more about you, and why you are here on earth. It is a desire that you have never had before. You begin to want to shift from the familiar places to a place of quiet so you can hear from God and gain understanding. You begin to feel a sense of energy and connectedness. You have a desire to become more authentic to yourself. You feel a sense of movement from wearing a mask to wanting to be your authentic self. Not everyone's systems are the same. However, everyone's systems will cause some level of discomfort. You begin to desire movement from a stagnant place concerning your purpose to a place of vision, even if you have not started moving. The awakening of purpose causes you to feel systems of change. You begin to question.

Your purpose can be awakened through various channels, including your pastor speaking a word from the Holy Spirit through reading His Word; you know, the "Ah ha" moment. Because God is a strategic God, no matter what, it all comes through the Holy Spirit using the best source of supply to reach you, which can be done through a vision, dream, revelation, or person, to name a few. Do not ignore the signs of change. This process will cause you to have to talk with the Great Physician, Christ. He will diagnose, redirect, and reposition you as you continue to make your appointment with Him. He will provide the right antidote and prescribe the right dosage of information to ensure that what you are birthing gets what it needs to fulfill the plan He has for you. Continue to consult Christ as you go through this new season of your life.

Awakening to Your Purpose

Awakening to your purpose is an exciting time in your life. You will begin to question your belief systems, practices, and how you live your life. It is what I call a wake-up call. Yes, the Holy Spirit wakes you up and allows you to pursue the call in your life. It is up to you to be in pursuit. After all, God gives us all a choice. As you decide to pursue your purpose in life, you begin to search for and learn even more about yourself. You begin to think about who you are around and reconsider connections with people and things that are distractions.

After speaking with various people who have faced challenges in their lives, I realized that each person desired to find their purpose and understand their destiny. They did not seem to know what their purpose or destiny was. This tells me they did not take the time in the face of God to draw closer to Him so the Holy Spirit could reveal it to them. One of the things that happens when you begin to move forward in the pursuit of your life's meaning is the shedding of immature and irresponsible behaviors. This allows you to recognize your worth and discover your life's purpose. The awakening of purpose is a stage of emotional adjustment and maturity. You have to go through the process of dealing with changing your perception of how life should be. You will do some soul searching as the Holy Spirit reconditions your way of thinking.

I experienced many of these things as I went through the awakening of my purpose. I can remember trying to determine my true identity and my life journey. Once you understand these two things, you will begin to feel a sense of maturity. Sometimes, I had to go into a quiet place to listen to obtain a download from the Holy Spirit. Other times, I had to get to know myself without the opinions of critics, naysayers, and haters. I had to embody the plan for my life. The change in maturity happened for me when I endured setbacks and had enough strength to weather the storm and get through the dangers of some pivotal moments in my life. It is never easy.

However, I suggest that as you take this journey, you start to work on removing the obstacles in your way. If you do not work on removing contaminated toxic beliefs, stereotypes, fears, the opinion of others, and false images of yourself, they can continue to cause self-identity issues. These challenges have the potential to stop you from discovering yourself.

Here are some ways to gain leverage as you maneuver through the process of inner soul searching and self-assurance. You must practice and adopt self-love and self-discovery to gain a sense of self-acceptance. You must learn to love yourself, no matter what you see. You have to begin to ask yourself, "What did God see?" You were created in His image to work toward being consistent and authentic to yourself. You will find that it is the easiest way to be, and you will regret the fact that you did not do it sooner. You find that you no longer feel the need to be a people-pleaser or carry the opinions of others on your shoulders. Instead, you embrace the new, revived energy that you have begun to accept. Making these changes will assist you and cause you to adjust and align with God's plan. Trust the process. Your end result is so worth the wait and perseverance.

Acceptance, Excitement, and Celebration

After you tap into your source through the Holy Spirit and accept that you have awakened your purpose, you are now ready to move into nurturing the gift God has given you. Pursuing and activating your God-given purpose is an inward connection and an outward experience that moves you into a place of pursuit; pursuing and activating your God-given purpose moves you closer to discovering its name. Your purpose has a name! You have to put in the time and connect with those who can assist you with that. If you do not put in the work, you will not carry out the plan through.

There will be more discussion as you move through future chapters. There is a surge through Christ using the Holy Spirit to speak and connect with you. There are times when the Holy Spirit gives you a revelation through others. Now you are another step closer to the delivery room. Stay in pursuit of your purpose, and do not grow weary in doing good, for in due season, you will reap if you do not give up (Galatians 6:9). However, this is only the first step to understanding the awakening. Remember that the labor pains will come sooner than you think. God will prepare you for the call on your life, which will require some stretching before you can be admitted for delivery.

Chapter Summary/Key Takeaways

Conception is all about connecting to a source of supply. Once you are connected to the Holy Spirit, the Holy Spirit begins to speak to you. The Holy Spirit is the connection between you and the Father. Conception is the start of life. Your purpose is defined and visible once you make God a priority.

1. You must connect to the Holy Spirit to obtain direction and insight from the Lord. The Holy Spirit is the connection to Christ.
2. You must awaken your purpose, or it will never grow or be birthed. You must recognize that your purpose is in a dormant state until you acknowledge it.
3. You must move. Once your purpose is stimulated, start moving forward so you do not lose momentum and your purpose stays undeveloped.

In the next chapter, you will understand how to go about discovering your God-given purpose. Yes, you will go into the discovery phase of birthing your purpose. We have talked about deepening our relationship with God. We discussed being intimate and making God your priority. As you begin to discover Christ, you begin to discover yourself, so hang in there because the intensity of what you are to birth will come at the appointed time.

CHAPTER 4

DISCOVERING YOUR PURPOSE

**Call to me and I will answer you and will
tell you great and hidden things that you
have not known. —Jeremiah 33:3**

Now that you understand why it is important to develop intimacy with God and how to find your identity in Christ, it is necessary to establish a relationship with Him so you become familiar with His voice. You have insight that you must go deeper into Him and have the faith of a mustard seed. As you become closer to Him, you will begin to trust Him enough to tell Him your secrets. You have come from a place of intimacy into the state of conception, where you put yourself in the position of awakening purpose through a divine connection. In the place of conception, you recognize that something is uncomfortable, something is out of alignment, something is not working right, something feels different, and you realize there is something inside you that is inactive, hidden, and needs to be activated.

Psalm 119:105 says, "Your word is a lamp to my feet and a light to my path." God's Word produces light in ways that may appear to be dark. The Bible tells you how to live a life that is pleasing to God. Living a God-filled life is the first step to discovering and identifying your purpose. You will learn that when you trust and follow Christ. Your direction and path become more apparent. When you become close to God, He begins to reveal your identity, and it is in your identity that you begin to learn more about yourself and more about God; you discover your purpose and awaken it. Your purpose has been resting inside you, so all this time, you have been walking around empty, wondering if you will ever find out what God has put inside of you. You have read that there must be an awakening and activation before you can birth your purpose. The purpose God puts inside you is to fulfill His plan on earth so He may get the glory out of your life.

Now you are in this phase of discovery. It has been revealed through previous chapters that something has been dormant in you for some time. You are in this place where you have gone through conception and intimacy, and you are now in the discovery stage. When your purpose is activated, you begin to experience the symptoms of something growing in you, and the diagnosis has been made. You are pregnant with your purpose. You are ready to pursue the identity of your calling and wonder how you will identify with your specific purpose. How do you function in a state of discovery, trying to fathom your purpose while pushing to make it through the process, as you begin to question areas of your life that you have never had to question? "What are the things I need to do?" and "What areas do I need to develop?" You begin to receive strength from the Father as you endure, walking through the process and discovering what God calls you to do. These questions will be answered as you read further in the book. If you are consistent in your search and growth in Christ, God will reveal your purpose to you.

God helps you to discover it. The Holy Spirit will speak to you. You have to be careful about listening to others when it comes to finding your calling. I say this because people can be out of alignment with what God has commissioned them to do. Make sure you seek God as it pertains to finding your reason for living. God knows you best. He created you in His image. Your call is valuable. It has meaning, so you must be careful about who you allow to speak into your life concerning your purpose, especially when you talk about the fact that God created you with a purpose and turn around and talk to those in the same situation as they help you identify with it. You must go to God about the discovery of your purpose.

Now let me be clear: It is not going to be easy. Once you are in the discovery phase, you have to invest. Investing in the birth of your calling is much greater than you think. Many people do not know what this means. Once you have uncovered the specific call on your life, you must begin to perfect it. Yes, it will cost a hefty price. It will cost you to read

God's Word, it will cost you time in prayer, it will cost you to read books to understand the call on your life, and it may cost you time away from social media platforms, people, places, and things. It will even cost you to stop feeling sorry for yourself and going back to dead places. God is not in your darkness. God is light. When going back to dark places in your life, God is not there. However, darkness is the place where the enemy wants to keep you. When you are in darkness, you cannot see. It is not until you come to know Christ that you receive sight.

Do you remember the empty tomb? Read John 20:11–18. Jesus was crucified and laid to rest in the tomb after His Crucifixion. In the morning hours, while it was still dark, Mary Magdalene went to the tomb with spices and noticed the stone had been removed from the entrance. She assumed that someone had taken Jesus's body. Mary was crying, and when she bent over to look into the tomb, she saw two angels in white garments where Jesus's body had been. One of the angels was seated at the head and the other at the foot.

To add to this, Mary ran to tell Simon Peter and the other disciples and said to them that someone had taken Jesus and she was unable to find Him. Peter and other disciples came to the tomb to confirm what Mary had told them. This is only one example of why you cannot continue to go back to the dark and dead places in your life. Mary was living in her past. She went back to the tomb because that was the last place she experienced hurt, pain, and death. It was a comfortable place for Mary. However, what she did not realize was that Jesus was not there. He was preparing to be with our Father in heaven. You continuously go back to dark places in life because it is comfortable. But remember, the absence of light is darkness. You have to decide if you want to live in light or darkness. God is light, and darkness is not of God. The enemy wants you to stay in this place.

> Your purpose has a name.
> ~Daphne Jett

Think about it: Mary was not only okay with returning to dark places to relive her pain and past hurts, but she also began to draw others into the darkness with her. Darkness is a place that stunts growth because, as long as you are in it, you cannot see your way out. It takes light to give you sight. God is not dead. He is alive. Therefore, you must embrace the light. To be with Him is to walk in His light.

Defining the call in your life and coming into alignment will take time. However, it is important that you find it and that you perfect that which God has given you to the best of your ability. Once you have uncovered the identity of your purpose, you have to prepare for your purpose to be birthed. When a woman finds out she is pregnant, she does not automatically know the gender of her baby. The fetus has to mature to at least eleven weeks old before the gender can be determined. The accuracy of determining your baby's gender increases with how far along you are in the pregnancy. The gender accuracy ranges from 70.3 percent at eleven weeks to 98.7 percent at twelve weeks to 100 percent at thirteen weeks (Brenner, D., MD, June 2021).The mother wants to know the gender of the baby so she can prepare before the birth. She understands that she must invest in the gift (the baby) before it arrives. It is no different from spiritual birth and maturity.

You must uncover the identity of your purpose and begin to mature in it. You will have to invest and prepare. What are the things you are going to have to give up? What are the things you are going to have to sacrifice? What are the things you will have to do that you usually would not do? What does your journey look like? Can you handle it? What are the things you will have to give up or surrender? What direction or path will you have to take? Do you need a GPS to guide you? You begin to question everything. Can you make it on your own? Know that God will guide you and give you answers to these questions. You may think that you are not built for this. I am here to tell you that you are built to make it to the end. You have to know how to put on the full armor of God as you go through this process and journey of discovery.

After you discover the identity of your purpose, you are going to walk into the delivery room and birth this gift. The stretching during labor and delivery is determined by the size of what God called you to birth. Prepare for the discomfort of what you will birth. The birth cannot happen if you have not been stretched enough to handle the size of what you will birth. It is not enough for me to go into discovery only based on the surface, with a lack of knowledge. Hosea 4:6 says, "My people are destroyed for lack of knowledge." Because you have rejected knowledge, "you must take the time to get understanding." You cannot skip over the process. What you carry will change the lives and hearts of many people. There is no time for surface assessment. You can listen to others tell you how their birth went. However, every delivery is different. The pain tolerance and size of what you birth may be different. It is not a one-size-fits-all when it comes to labor. You cannot go into the birthing room with a thousand-dollar mindset when you are birthing a billion-dollar promise. You must take heed to what I am sharing with you.

You do not have time for surface gauging. You must keep the Word of God in your daily agenda and the Holy Spirit nearby. Protect your ears and heart from opinions and tactics that have no value in comparison to what you have. This is the stage where you have to drown out the noise. I am glad you asked: the noise of people who are struggling to find out who they are. They are not walking in the call God has for them. However, because what they say to you sounds good, you think you are receiving it from them, not realizing it is a trap set to take you off course. It could potentially cause you to birth your gift prematurely, and now you have to deal with the complications because you listened to someone else's opinion and not to Christ, Who is the creator of all things.

Listen. This thing is about you and God. When you are connected to Him through the Holy Spirit, you will know when He sends people who are there to help you through the process. That comes with discernment and wisdom. This birth is about the Kingdom of God. There is no greater love than discovering your purpose. There is no greater love than walking in the fullness of all God has called you to do in this life. There is a blessing in seeking out your identity. Miracles, signs, and wonders begin to happen when you start to move forward in the obedience of God. When you start moving forward, you will run into the identity of what you will birth in your birthing season. As you stay on course with discovery, it will cause you to want Him more, and you will develop an everlasting friendship with God the Father. When you stay on course and focused, there is a level of endurance, strength, and development taking place in you. It prevents you from breaking it. You become immune to things that come to distract you.

Identifying the name of your purpose is better than going back to a dormant state. At this point, you are like a willow tree. You may bend, but you will not break. The process is not going to be easy. But identifying your God-given purpose will be worth it. However, it will cost you something. I want to let you in on the Word of God. While purpose is being spoken over every platform, and it feels good and excites you, Hebrews 11:13 says, "Many people of faith died not having received the promises of God, but having seen them from afar, were assured of them, and embraced them." So, millions of people from around the world came to believe in Jesus Christ, but they did not receive the things God promised them when they died. You must put in the work, and it will cost. You must stay on course and remember your why. The lives of people are waiting at bay for your purpose to be born so they can obtain the freedom, edification, and comfort that only you can provide. You have a purpose as long as you have breath. Yes, your life has meaning. You have to be bold about who you are.

Have you ever heard the expressions "If only you knew what God had put inside of you" or "If only you knew how great you are"? It is so true, even when you do not believe it. You have to renew your mind so when you see yourself, you see greatness. You are uniquely made. You are designed to complete the tasks God has planned for you while on earth. There are times you allow your past, your shame, your disappointments, and what people have said about you, true or false, to distort how you see yourself. When your vision is distorted, it causes your vision to be blurry and keeps you from seeing your greatness. Blurred vision keeps you from seeing what God has put inside you. It has become distorted by the tactics and tricks of the enemy. Just like God uses people to bless you, he also uses people to speak into your life to empower you, push you, and equip you through the Holy Spirit.

It is the same for the enemy. He sends people to curse you, even when they do not know they are doing it, you must know who God says you are. You may feel inadequate, as if you do not feel you are the best looking, you may feel as though you are not the most elite. However, you are a son or daughter of the highest God. You must acknowledge your greatness because God is great and created you in His image. You have unique gifts to help you walk in all that God has purposed and called you to be. You must know your worth. You must understand that you are more than enough, no matter what you see. Seek after Him with all your might and all your strength. Run to Him like never before. Help others find Him so they may discover who they are and why they are here.

Discovering your gift, as discussed, is so important. God has given some people insight into your calling. They can see the call in your life and have the ability to identify with what that call is. Many times, you are unable to identify with your purpose because you are caught up in your own thoughts. Get out of your way! Be thankful that God loves you enough to allow others to see your gifts and bring you into the knowledge of why you are called. Your purpose has a name, and once you discover it, continue to prepare to move forward so you can impact the lives of others.

The Process of Discovery

It is understandable if the idea of learning God's plan for your life makes you feel lost. You may believe that you already know which path to take. You, on the other hand, are afraid of making a mistake. It does not have to be difficult to follow God's plan for your life. He wants to show you your purpose. Proverbs 20:27 states, "The spirit of man is the candle of the Lord, searching all the inward parts of the heart."

God wants to show you things about your future, but He does not want to do so through Instagram, Facebook, Snapchat, reality television, or any other form of social media. He wants one on one time with you. As a result, it is critical to form a relationship with Christ through the Holy Spirit. The truth is that hearing God is not difficult; nonetheless, you must learn to recognize His voice, be silent, listen, and pay attention in order to hear Him. When you are preoccupied with a lot of other things that you have prioritized over God, it is difficult to stay focused on Him. I understand that social media is far more enjoyable than reading your Bible and praying. On the other hand, God wants to speak with you and disclose things to you. All you have to do now is get quiet and listen to your spirit.

When you have that fact firmly embedded in your heart, it will be easy to find. God wants to tell you about His intentions for your life. He wants to help you make informed decisions about your future. Those realities are spoken to your spirit by God. If you remain silent and open to listening, God will show you how to take the next step. For Jeremiah 29:11 states, "'For I know the plans that I have for you,' says the Lord, 'plans for peace and not for evil, to give you a future and a hope.'"

Developing a relationship with God is all about getting to know Him better. As you spend time in the Bible and in prayer, you will get to know the things God likes and understand His hopes and dreams for you. You will find Him; the Bible reveals God has something special in mind for you. And it is His desire to reveal them to you. All you have to do now is strengthen your relationship with God. Spend time in His presence. Seek Him out. The Bible promises you will find Him. You would want to spend time with someone you are dating to get to know them better. You would want to know everything about their preferences and desires. It is no different when it comes to cultivating a connection with God. It all comes down to taking the time to get to know Him. As you spend time in the Bible and in prayer, you will discover what God likes and what His hopes and dreams are for you.

Did you realize that your purpose is different from your identity? What exactly do I mean? What I stated was exactly what I meant. Your identity in Christ is not defined by your purpose. I recall attending a meeting where each individual in the room had to introduce themselves to the rest of the group. When it was my turn to speak, I introduced myself and gave my job title as Senior Manager over a group of 22 employees. Everyone was taken aback since they had no idea, I was a leader in this capacity. Over the next two to three months, I started receiving emails asking if I was available for a coffee chat. People would approach me and ask if I would mentor them because they heard I was the woman to talk to based on a career title. However, they did not realize that my title was not my identity.

Society as a whole place far too much importance on what people do for a living. It occurs frequently enough that it becomes a person's identity. Someone approached me and said, "Hi, Daphne, I am Tina, the CMO." People place much too much value on job titles, yet a person's profession is not their identity. Jesus is the source of your identity. Find out what Jesus has to say about you in the Bible. Allow who you are in Christ to become your identity. Jesus is who you are. God wants you to be successful in all aspects of your life. He cares more about you knowing who you are in Christ than what you end up doing for a living. So, during the discovery process, spend some time focusing on what God says about you. Recognize that God desires for you to prosper in all areas of your life.

You may not see your abilities right away. It is up to you to figure out what you are good at and study it. Learning what you are not excellent at is a crucial step in determining what you are. Maintain your efforts to learn more about yourself and your abilities. You might find that while you enjoy volunteering with children's ministry at your church, working with the media team is something you loathe. That is okay. You are on a quest to learn more about yourself. You are always discovering new things about yourself and your talents and abilities. Participate in the activities of your local church. Once you start serving in your church or volunteering in your community, you will begin to notice the things you are good at doing and the things you are not so good at doing. It is all part of the learning process. The more you learn, the better you will become.

It takes some work to discover your purpose, but God wants to reveal your destiny to you. Both spending time with God and learning about yourself and your life's purpose are essential. If you choose to spend time with Him and listen, He will speak to your spirit and reveal to you the next steps to take. It is a guarantee that God will carry out His plan for you. I strongly suggest you spend some time with Him. By establishing your unique vision and recognizing your comparative advantage, you can consider how you can use our gifts and talents for God's purposes. It also requires comprehending the how and why of effectively applying these God-given abilities in daily life. God has entrusted you with certain resources, talents, and capacities. It is your responsibility to maintain that trust by managing these matters appropriately, in accordance with His wishes. Christians must use their talents and endowments in ways that are consistent with God's design and desire. You are expected to be a decent person in everything you do. Unfortunately, many Christians go to work with the mindset that their abilities exist solely to allow them to acquire a huge sum of money and retire. God gave you your abilities to help others rather than to enrich yourself. And God has given you the powers of others. What can you do to make a difference in the lives of others? Your gift was not intended for you. Others are meant to benefit from your abilities.

Investing in Your Purpose

The discovery phase of purpose is identifying the call on your life. It does not have to be hard to discover your call, but you also have to invest in understanding the call. Proverbs 18:16 says, "A man's gift makes room for him and brings him before great men." This scripture is a powerful statement. What you were designed to be known for is your gift. God has put a gift or talent in every person that the world will make room for. This gift will enable you to fulfill your vision. You must invest and plan because what is maturing inside you will often have an impact on nations, so you must care for it as if it has already been born. Your preparation prepares you for the stretching as you get further along, preparing your mind and body to be able to handle the birth. You will read more about stretching in Chapter 9.

It is vital that you invest in your gift; you may see you have a gift but think it is too far away or too big for you to comprehend. You come to the conclusion that while you want to pursue your gift, you feel unworthy of it or incapable of handling it; thus, you decide to back out of the promise. Please do not avoid the promise. Do not avoid it because you feel incapable of carrying it out or you do not believe you have the skills or knowledge to help it grow. I always tell people to take their feelings out and deal with the facts. Do not think out of your pain because it causes you to make decisions you would not make when you are healthy. You have to understand your greatness in God. Understanding your greatness in God means you have to ensure your inner beliefs align with God's Word.

Mark Twain said, "The most important days in your life are the day you are born and the day you find out why." So, evaluate your underlying morals, ethics, and faith. This means you must check your belief system. It is critical that you connect with God and understand your true identity in Christ. Your true identity starts with getting to know Him. Because He has created you with a purpose, He knows you best. He will reveal it so you understand it and know it is from Him, as discussed in chapter 2. Think about the various values. Think about your beliefs and what you desire to improve as you live out this life God has given you. Many times, you discover insights in these answers as you continue to read God's Word and go before the Lord in prayer.

Have you ever had a dream that motivates you from the inside out? Seeking out the reason you are here on earth should open your heart and build perseverance. Seeking your identity should inspire you from the inside out. Get out of your own way. It is so important to get out of your own way so you can deal with your fears, overcome your challenges, and get rid of the things that limit your thinking. What you believe and how you believe are two sides of the same coin. Write down some of the things that cause you to fear. This helps you get back to the core of your values and beliefs and understand what you believe and why you believe it. Ask yourself if your beliefs align with the Word of God. If they do not, I suggest praying and working toward shifting your mindset. Train your mind to think differently. You have to limit beliefs and fears that prevent you from producing positive results.

Unfortunately, many of our fears and negative thoughts are subconsciously built over the course of your life and stem from things that happen in childhood. These things build insecurities and cause you to question what God said about you. The Bible teaches you about who you are; you just have to believe it. And you have the power of God, which means you can speak things that are not as though they are. You can speak to a situation, and it has to respond to your command. Mark 11:23 states, "For truly I say to you, whoever says to this mountain, 'Be removed and be thrown into the sea,' and does not doubt in his heart, but believes that what he says will come to pass, he will have whatever he says." These are some of the things that happen when you understand the power of God that rests in you. When you speak it and have faith, your words cause whatever you have spoken in faith to respond to the command you have given. You must believe it because God gave you the power.

God is instructing you that you should not doubt in your hearts, which really means you should believe God's Word without needing proof because you trust Him. Not trusting God from the inside out causes you to miss God. Yes, you miss Him, and what happens is you abandon the blessing or the promise at the point of its deliverance when fear and negative thoughts hold precedence over our faith in Christ. Also, the willingness to keep His Word and understand that His Word never returns void, that whatever God sends His Word to do, it must be done.

I challenge you to start speaking life and prophesying over yourself, identifying and discovering who you are in Christ. If you begin to declare and speak it into the atmosphere and believe that it will come to pass, you will be able to manifest it. You will begin to see the unveiling of who you are and Who Christ is in you. He will reveal how He wants to use you on earth. You must stop believing negative words and things that others have said when they have no value in your life and are not enhancing who God has called you to be. When there are words spoken over you that do not align with God's Word, you have to rebuke them. I do not care about those from whom it is coming. Those who love you will see that which God has called you to, and if there is something that needs to be corrected when it is from God, it is done in love. Why? Because the Holy Spirit is a gentleman, when it is from the Holy Spirit, it is always done in love, because God is love. You have to know when to rebuke.

Break seals that have never been broken in your family through pushing yourself into the uncomfortable when it is warranted. You have to know when to go deeper when you have to go far beyond the surface of what you set out to accomplish. Learning who you are will take soul searching. However, it will take movement and investment in you by learning and gaining instructions. Harriet Tubman said, "Every great dream begins with a dreamer." Always remember that you have within you the strength, the patience, and the passion to reach for the stars to change the world. God called you and provided you with everything you needed.

There are two scriptures that come to mind: He calls whom He chooses and then equips them. He really does choose those who seem inadequate or weak in this world. So, you do not have to be perfect and have it all together. In fact, in 1 Corinthians 1:26–29, Paul reminds you to "observe your calling, brothers. Among you, there were not many wise men, according to the flesh, many mighty men, and many noble men. But God has chosen the foolish things of the world to confound the wise. For God has chosen the weak things of the world to confound the mighty. And God has chosen the base things of the world and things that are despised. Yes, and He chose things that did not exist to bring about anything that does, so that no flesh should boast in His presence."

When Kevin and I found out I was pregnant with our son, we did not know the first thing about being parents. However, we began to ask the doctor questions and talked to our close friends who we thought were good parents. We also asked our mothers questions about parenting. Most importantly, we discussed our life experiences from childhood.

God begins to give you wisdom. I read books and magazines about parenting, which gave me more insight into birthing a child. One of the things I understood was that only God gives life. When you become pregnant, at an appointed time, God gives you everything you need to be a mother. Romans 8:28–30 says, "You know that all things work together for good for those who love God, for those who are called according to His purpose. He predestined those he foreknew to be conformed to the image of His Son, so that he could be the firstborn among many brothers. And those He predestined, He also called; those He called, He also justified; and those He justified, He also glorified." I am thankful to know that this is the Word of the Lord.

The Revealing of Your Gift

In light of God allowing, you to discover your gift, there needs to be forward movement. When you get to a state where you feel God is leading you to find your purpose, it is time to get started moving forward. Do not stay stagnant in a place of fear. Move. Even if you have some reservations or are unsure, move. You cannot afford to wait for things to be perfect. However, God will direct you and provide instruction. As you begin to move, He will become your GPS. As you invest quality time in understanding the call of God in your life, make sure you are connecting with people who are dear to you from a spiritual standpoint. Check to see if they understand your calling and are willing to mentor you. They must be willing to invest in you. You may want a mentor or spiritual parent to guide you on this journey of discovery. Investing in yourself and moving in pursuit of your knowledge as it concerns your purpose is not easy, and just like driving a car, the farther you go, the more gas you use. I ask that no matter how far the journey is, do not give up. Use God as your GPS. His route will get you straight to your destination, right on time. Remember, this new journey can be exciting when you begin to move.

However, as with anything, the excitement begins to wane, depending on the journey. Do not give up. Do not listen to distractions. Do not listen to negativity. Guard your heart. If it is not from God, bind it and rebuke it. Do not give up. "It is the season that you will reap the harvest of what you have planted if you do not faint (Galatians 6:9). You cannot afford to stay stagnant and complacent. Philippians 3:12–14 tells you to "forget those things which are behind and reach forward to those things which are ahead, and to press toward the goal for the prize of the high calling of God in Christ Jesus." Continue to press forward. It does not matter whether you hop, skip, or jump. Continue to press, even if it is uncomfortable. Stay focused with your mind on the end goal, until you begin to see the manifestation of all God has for you. Being obedient to what God has called you to do allows you to walk out your purpose and share it with others so they may have life.

No matter where you are on this journey, learn to distinguish the voice of God. John 10:27 says, "My sheep hear My voice, and I know them, and they follow Me." When you follow Christ, you should be able to recognize His voice when you hear it. This is why it is valuable to become intimate with Him. If you do not know His voice, confusion steps in, takes you off course, and puts you out of alignment with the plan of God.

You know, God is not a God of confusion. You must spend time in the Word of God. The Bible says, "So then faith comes by hearing, and hearing by the word of God" (Romans 10:17). You have to listen and tune your ears to hear what the Lord says. As I stated before, you must work to invest in developing and strengthening your gift. You must get out of your own way. You cannot be in control. Pray for God to take control and speak to you.

Get out of the way. Let go and allow God to give you directions. Without His guidance, there may be many setbacks. I can tell you from experience that it is not easy, but I will say that releasing it to God will be worth it, as you develop the skills to know about your calling. God will make His gifts known to you. He must be your first priority, and His will must take precedence over all other considerations. Nothing can happen without God's ordaining it. Psalm 57:2 says, "I will cry to God Most High, to God who vindicates me." Understanding God's plan is vital. Your days are numbered. God will fulfill every purpose and plan for you. However, He gives you a choice. It is up to you to do the work and move forward with what He has called you to do on earth. You must move.

Chapter Summary/Key Takeaways

To live with a God-given purpose, you must first lay down your life in order to acquire life. God has better plans for us than we can fathom, and He does things we do not comprehend, but we must trust in His will. There are various strategies for living a purpose-driven life that we can learn from scripture. God is God, and everything He does, including everything in your life, is for His purposes. Nothing can happen unless God permits it. Psalm 57:2 says, "I cry out to God Most High, to God who fulfills his purpose for me." This is key in understanding God's purpose for your life. The scripture tells us how to find your purpose:

1. Read your Bible. God reveals Himself to us, and we can discover our true identity in Him.
2. Pray to God, requesting that He reveal His plan for your life. Request that He show you and provide you with clarity.
3. Listen carefully to hear God's voice. He wants to talk to you.

Drown out the noise of your past. You have been carrying an identity that is not from God for far too long. Renew your thoughts, and believe what Jesus says about you as you move forward in Christ. Chapter 5 is about nurturing the gift God has given you. It will provide insight on how to take on a new mind and break old habits and soul ties. You must be willing to release yourself from life's past disappointments so you can experience God's freedom.

CHAPTER 5

SPIRITUAL NURTURING

I have fed you with milk and not with solid
food. For to this day, you were not able
to endure it. Nor are you able now.
—1 Corinthians 3:2

Now that you have gone through various stages in birthing the promise of God, you will embark upon some critical steps within this process. When God reveals your gift to you and you begin to invest, you are just starting to move into the more critical stages. Your promise is developing from the time conception is connected. So, the bigger the promise, the heavier the weight. You are at a stage where you have to nurture different areas of your life.

I know you believe that purpose just happens once you discover it, but that is not the case. This is when mothers seek to learn more about their pregnancy. They read books for baby names, look for baby furniture, prepare the room for the baby, and tell the people closest to them about their pregnancy. They speak with their doctor to get the proper nutrients during pregnancy. They go to the doctor at every stage of their pregnancy. They seek the Holy Spirit to obtain the information they need as they move forward in nurturing their gift and preparing for labor and delivery. Matthew 7:7 says, "Ask and it will be given to you; seek and you will find; knock and it will be opened to you." God will provide, but you must be willing to go after it.

When you and your significant other become pregnant, you begin to prepare. What are the things you need to do? What does parenthood look like? How will this change your lives? How will it affect your time with family, friends, and colleagues? There are many other questions. Even through these preparations, some things will be missed. As I stated in previous chapters, there will always be unexpected things as you finish this journey, and that is okay. We all experience it. However, mothers do some basic things to prepare. It is vital to plan.

You will notice similarities when you begin to nurture the gift. Though the time has not yet arrived, you must prepare for the hospital visit. As you begin this process, you may be worried or nervous about birthing the promise, knowing that with birthing this, God has expectations of you, and you are held accountable to fulfill His plan. As you get closer, preparing to give birth to your gift may be overwhelming because of your responsibility and its significance. It can be life-altering. Think about Mary and Joseph. I can only imagine the plans they had for their life together. However, God had other plans for her. Joseph was not ready to take on the responsibility of a woman pregnant by someone else, and Mary could not understand why God chose her.

As you begin this phase, I suggest you follow what is called the "Stop, Start, and Continue Method" (Ciccarelli, "Start, Stop, Continue Tutorial."). In this technique, which I used in my corporate career, you look back at what you did and decide if these are things that should continue to exist as you move forward with planning. Now is the time to take inventory. It is imperative to the birth of what you have going on inside you. Once you discover your purpose, it will help you highlight those things that will help you enhance, invest, and strengthen your knowledge of your purpose.

Taking on a New Mind

You have to change your mindset. You can no longer think the same way. When you know better, you must strive to become better in every aspect of your life. It is impossible to keep doing the same thing and expect

> When you recondition your thoughts and your way of thinking, it can change the trajectory of everything that goes on around you and your perspective of it.
> ~Daphne Jett

different results. Romans 12:2 says, "Do not be conformed to this world, but be transformed by the renewing of your mind, that you may prove what is the good and acceptable and perfect will of God."

Taking on a new mindset can be challenging because you have always done things a certain way for so many years; you have always thought about things in a specific way, and this may be how it has been since birth. So, it makes sense to me. Well, just because you have been doing it that way for some time, or because that is your belief, or because that is how your parents raised you, it does not mean it will work in this season of your life. You must adjust your thinking to where you are going, not to where you have been. Old things have passed away, and you are in the season of newness. You must renew your mind to make it to labor and delivery.

Now is the time. It is going to be hard to change, especially when it has been your way of thinking for your lifetime. However, it is necessary and imperative to the growth of what you carry. God's intention was not for you to take on the world's way of doing things. Hebrews 10:38 tells us, "Now the just shall live by faith; but if anyone draws back, my soul shall have no pleasure in him." God's intention was for you to live by faith. You are to live by faith and not by sight, because faith is the substance of things hoped for and the evidence of things not seen. You cannot please God without having faith. You must trust and believe He will reward you as you seek Him.

God is seeking people of faith. When you recondition your thoughts and your way of thinking, it can change the trajectory of everything that goes on around you and your perspective of it. Yes, you can literally change the world. You can change your situation. Remember the commercial back in the 1980s that said, "A mind is a terrible thing to waste"? It is so true. Your mind is powerful. Your mind is so powerful, it can bring life or death to a situation because everything you do in life starts with a thought. Look at it this way: Something has to come to your mind before you decide if it is something you want to believe.

Before you speak about it or act on what you are thinking, wait. There are too many people walking around in poverty or in a secondary mindset. If your mind does not change, you live in the capacity of your thinking. You will remain within the constraints of your thinking until you change how you think, no matter how much you desire. You must get out of your own way. That is why it is important to know who you are in Christ. Do not be the person I used to be. I would say I knew who I was on the surface, but in my quiet place with God, I was so broken; I was insecure and wanted to give up. However, when I found out who I was in Christ, I came to understand my why and other truths about myself. I was able to deal with my shortcomings and the things that caused me harm and pain. Yes, I had to deal with the pain, but after I established a relationship with Christ, I began to understand who I was and aligned with who God said I was.

There are too many Christians out here doing themselves a disservice by playing what I call "surface ball." Surface ball is when people have all the accolades, know the scriptures in the Bible, understand how to play church, but there is no substance, and there is no biblical foundation of knowing who they are in Christ. They do not have the ability to adopt the scriptures they quote. They just know the church because they practice it. They have lived in a playing church environment for decades, so they do not realize they are playing surface ball and are still in a place of limitations, no further than the surface of what their minds contain. However, they do not yet know God from an intimate standpoint. There has to be humility, and people must want to know Him more and me aside for Him.

Surface Christians just want to be seen; they do not have a servant's heart or a desire to know God. Their desire to serve God must be stronger than their agenda. He is the Word. Knowing His Word is knowing Him. They must desire to develop a true relationship and a true identity with Him so their purpose may be fulfilled, so they may meet their destiny, and so God's glory may be revealed in every situation He puts them in.

You must renew your minds so you can align with your true identity in Christ. You must learn who you are in Him on the inside so that what is on the outside aligns and agrees with what is on the inside. It reflects what comes out. There is an old saying that what you put in, at some point, will come out. God called the Pharisees hypocrites in Matthew 23:13. The Pharisees were materialistic, pleasure-seeking, self-indulging, and greedy. They presented the appearance of righteousness and were honorable keepers of the law. However, they were not righteous on any account. They wore the mask of righteousness, but their internal, hidden world consisted of ungodly thinking and evil spirits. Their viewpoints were out of alignment with the things of God. They wore disguises.

A new mind has nothing to do with how well you dress, how well you speak, what college you attended, or how many degrees you hold. It has everything to do with who God has created you to be on earth and how you are fulfilling the plan. In 1 Samuel 16:7, the Lord says, "Do not look at His appearance or at the height of His stature, because I have rejected Him. Because the LORD does not see as man does. For man looks at the outward appearance, but the LORD looks at the heart." Don't you want God to accept you? I know I do. I want God to be pleased with how I handle the gifts and assignments He has given me.

People will perceive you as one thing and pass judgment, not realizing that they will meet hell first. They allow their mind to dictate to them their innermost being and thoughts. Be careful, be incredibly careful about your mind. Your mind can destroy what it sees. That is why you have to be careful about perceiving people in a certain way. David's Psalm 110 says, "Sit at my right hand until I make your enemies a footstool [which is a throne for your feet]. The Lord will extend your mighty scepter from Zion. You will rule in the midst of your enemies. Your troops will be willing on your day of battle."

Do you realize that the enemy wants your mind and anything attached to it? He does not want anything that is not attached to the mind. If your mind is attached to things, then he wants your things. Protect and control the thoughts of your mind, and make sure when you decide what to do with your thoughts that your decisions are made based on the mindset, "Is it going to please God?"

Make the decision to turn into the person God says you are. At the end of the day, it does not matter what people say or think about you. What matters is how you view yourself. If you are a surface ballplayer, stop being a hollow shell that has nothing internal or external to protect it when the enemy sends its camp. As soon as something is thrown at you, it will break because there is nothing but a shell keeping you together. You are fortunate God allows you to make choices. He has given you the ability to gain knowledge, to think for yourself, and to use wisdom and logic, which is what makes you human.

Your thoughts, ideas, and beliefs reflect who you are. God recognizes this and talks about these things throughout the Bible. One passage that comes to mind is "for as he thinks in his heart, so is he. 'Eat and drink!' he says to you, but His heart is not with you" (Proverbs 23:7).

Proverbs 23:7 reflects on someone who says one thing, but their heart is so far from what they say. Their hearts are in a different place than what they say. Therefore, it is like a puzzle. It makes it hard to determine what you should believe. I believe what is in my heart. Because the views of your thoughts, your feelings, and your heart form the reality of who you are. The Bible says that it is out of the mouth that the heart speaks, which means you have to decide if you will give your heart access to the things you believe are good or bad. If it is in your heart, it will be revealed through your mouth. However, you do not realize that it displays and exposes who you are. It really shapes how you think, which in turn shapes your behaviors and forms the foundation of your thinking, which becomes who you are. Needless to say, as you pursue your God-given purpose, you must shift the way you think and take on a godly mindset. God wants you to embrace a Christlike mindset.

A Christlike mindset removes you from acting out of a worldly way of thinking. When you have a Christlike mindset, you begin to understand Christ, and in turn, you respond to the behaviors described in the word of God. As you work to change your way of thinking, God will provide you with the grace and guidance you need to work out your thoughts as you draw closer to Him. As you become one with Him in spirit and in truth, there is a level of humility and submission that must be present as you walk through, shifting from a worldly or negative view to a Christlike and positive view. Your mindset is the thought framework that clarifies how you figure out life situations and make decisions. God's will for your life is for you to have the mind of Christ. To understand the mind of God is to seek His Word.

You must break the habits you have. Some habits you have had since your youth, and some you adopt by the things you are attached to. You must move away from the phrases, "This is just how I am," and "I am just keeping it real." First, saying this is just how you are does not require you to make a change for the better. When you say, "This is just how I am," you do not realize God wants you to be more than who you are. Second, being who you are does not help anyone, not even yourself. However, God wants you to be who He designed you to be. When you become who God says you are, you have the power and authority to trample on serpents and scorpions, over all the power of the enemy, and not be hurt by them. Read Luke 10:19. This is when our thoughts and hearts align with the word of God.

When you say, "I am just keeping it real," what you are saying is, "This is my way of hurting you based on my perception of you." However, you do not realize this is just your opinion. "Keeping it real" is a negative way your heart is being exposed, because those attached to your calling will speak life. They will not speak of death or negativity. People who keep it real only find negativity in situations.

Breaking Old Habits

You have to remove yourself from various situations and ways of doing things. You have to adopt a new way of thinking. You can no longer think like the world. Taking on a new mind provided you with insight on how to move from the world's viewpoint to a Christlike mind. Before we go any further, I want to tell you that three things are needed in order to keep a Christ-like mind:

1. Discipline, consistency, practice, and stripping off the things and people who do not align with God's Word and your newness. I must say, this is not easy.
2. You must enforce and reinforce until your new mindset is obedient to your new way of thinking. Because your flesh will fight you to go back into those old habits, practice discipline.
3. You must carry it out and perform it until it becomes a habit. Yes, you must rehearse it repeatedly until it eventually becomes ingrained in your behavior. Just as you did for the world, you must have the same persistence to do the right things in Christ, so practice it until it becomes your reality.

There are so many things you will see when you come to know who you are, and as you shift and begin to see the world through the lens of Christ, talk about it. When a mother finds out the gender of her unborn child, she begins to prepare for birthing a healthy baby. She begins to evaluate her eating habits. She is careful about being around sick people. She stops these habits, such as drinking, smoking, partying, and anything that could cause harm to her and the unborn child. She begins to have doctor visits to guard against infections or other health issues. She begins to add things to her life, such as prenatal vitamins and a healthier way of living, which includes being healthier physically and mentally. Set time aside to pray and study God's Word because you are medicated through the downloading of the Holy Spirit. This is when you can go to the Father and tell Him how you feel. Talk to Him about any uncommon symptoms you are experiencing. This is where you will obtain instruction, take the information, and start applying it. You will begin to gain strength and endurance to keep going.

When nurturing your gift, you have to "put off the former way of life in the old nature and be renewed in the spirit of your mind; and that you put on the new nature, which was created according to God in righteousness and true holiness" (Ephesians 4:22–24). You have to prepare for what is to come. Do not think the enemy is going to allow you to bring forth your gift with ease. That is not going to happen. He will try anything to take you off course and distract you. So whatever God prescribes to you during your prayer and study time, make sure you follow the instructions. Be prepared to listen. It is critical to the outcome of what you carry.

At this point, mothers shift their minds to birthing healthy babies. They want to make sure they do not miscarry or have the baby prematurely. They want to make the right decisions; that is why they changed from their old way of thinking and put on a new mindset to support the healthy needs of the child.

When I was pregnant, I remember shifting my mindset to align with motherhood. I now had another life to attend to. I knew it was going to be different for both myself and my husband. Kevin had to shift his mindset to include what he would have to ensure as I carried our child. There was a patience that he had to have to tolerate me at that point. Okay, Kevin's shifting way of thinking was one of the first things he had to adjust to. Needless to say, you both have to make changes to how you think.

I interviewed Kevin as I wrote this book. I asked him to give me insight from a man's perspective on his thoughts when he found out I was pregnant, especially since he was not the one carrying the baby. I was in awe of his answers because they were different than what I was thinking. Kevin said he had to shift his mind from being in a place providing for himself and his wife to thinking about how he would care for an additional person, his child. He thought about the fact that he was becoming a father and the impact of the change that was about to come into his life. Could he handle it? Was he ready? How about the fact that having a child would take away his freedom, and he would have to mature as a man much faster because of the responsibility (especially since we had our child so young)? The last point he gave was the reality that he had a son coming into the world, and he had to provide for and protect himself, his child, and his wife. Being pregnant with a purpose is no different than seeking to begin anything else in life.

As you prepare to birth the promise of God, your God-given purpose, you will begin to look at the things that conflict or cause friction with having the mind of Christ. Many of the things you will identify with during the growth period are things you would not have ever been able to see with a worldly mindset. Many times, looking at things through the eyes of the world causes you to have blurry vision. The enemy would never allow you to see the things God has for you. He never wants you to fulfill the things you were born to do. Once you take on the mind of Christ, you no longer have blurry vision. God gives you clear vision to carry out His plans for your life.

The first thing you want to do is think about the things you did today that you know God would not be pleased with. They could cause harm to your destiny. For example, when I found out I was pregnant with my purpose, I had to deal with some past hurt, pain, disappointment, and shame that I carried for many years. I knew that in order for me to birth my purpose, I had to ensure that I was in a healthy space and that I was effective in doing what God needed me to do. I had to forgive. What I am saying is that there were people, places, and things I was attached to. I had it, and it had me. You know what those places are, and as you continue to walk in your newness in Christ, He will reveal them to you. It is going to be hard because "we wrestle not against flesh and blood, but against principalities, against powers, against the rulers of the darkness of this world, against spiritual wickedness in high places" (Ephesians 6:12).

There is a time and place for everything. Ecclesiastes 3:1–8 states there is a season for everything (just know that your season may not be someone else's season): "To everything, there is a season, a time for every purpose under heaven: a time to be born, and a time to die; a time to plant, and a time to uproot what is planted; a time to kill, and a time to heal; a time to break down, and a time to build up; a time to weep, and a time to laugh; a time to mourn, and a time to dance; a time to cast away stones, and a time to gather stones; a time to embrace, and a time to refrain from embracing; a time to gain, and a time to lose; a time to keep, and a time to cast away; a time to tear, and a time to sew; a time to keep silence, and a time to speak; a time to love, and a time to hate; a time of war, and a time of peace." This passage lets me know that everything in life is meaningless, separated from God. You can make every effort to achieve just about anything you desire. However, if it is not with the intent of glorifying God and for your own selfish purpose, it will not have a long-lasting sense of fulfillment. Be sure that whatever you do, you do it to glorify God the Father.

Nonvalue Adds in the Process

Now that you are clear on what the seasons may bring and know that you must have a renewed mind, I will say this process is not easy. Let us get down to the breaking and releasing of things that have been. As you move into a new way of thinking, there are things you have carried for so long that you do not realize continue to hinder you from moving forward. There are people you have been attached to for so long that you have to decide if the relationship is worth keeping. There are also places you have been that open you up to being hurt. The unfortunate part is that you stay connected to these things because you understand them, and they are comfortable. Now you are at the place where I have to pose a question. How badly do you want it? How much are you willing to sacrifice to see your purpose fulfilled to its fullest potential? What are you willing to give up so you can see the promises of God moving in your life? You have arrived at the point where the enemy is concerned; this is where you evaluate personal attachments that no longer fit where you are going.

There is a period of disconnecting and cutting ties with people, places, and things that have a negative impact on your life. Many of these things are connected to ties you have allowed to get knotted. Have you ever tried to tie a pair of shoes but the shoelace got a knot in it? Trying to get the knot out of the shoelace can be almost impossible. So, in life, you have become tied or connected to places, to people, and to stuff that prevents you from moving forward in the things of God. These are merely stumbling blocks that prevent you from seeing the manifestation of what God has prophesied over your life. These things are known as "soul ties."

Soul ties are not something new. Soul ties have the power to manipulate, influence, and control you even when they are not aware they are playing this role. There are times when they do not realize they are doing it. When you allow others to take ownership and dictate your moves and actions, it is unhealthy for you and for them to move forward with fulfilling your purpose. If you want to move forward, you need to leave them alone and move on. Listen, it does not matter how long you have known a person. It could be five minutes or fifty years. If people are not adding value to your life, let them go. They could be the very thing keeping you from moving forward. Ask God to begin connecting you with people who understand what you carry and can assist you on your journey of following Christ and fulfilling God's plan in your life.

Some people think that soul ties can be good or bad. They are referred to as "spiritual connections." They are usually formed after a deeply close spiritual, intimate, or emotional relationship. A soul tie happens when someone has a strong influence on your life for a significant period of time, such that an unhealthy bond is formed. Even after you end the relationship, the bond and hunger to be around that person may persist. How about your favorite place to go? Even though you know it is not good for you to be there, the urge to still be there is winning. If you do not end an intense relationship, the connection can stay attached to you for many years.

I can remember the conviction I felt as I continued to move toward pursuing my purpose. There were people who were a weight in my life. There were things I carried with me for many years that I should have left a long time ago. However, I needed to hang on to the weight because it was my excuse to not move forward. It was my protection from not doing what I knew I should have done a long time ago. When you pursue your purpose, there are people you will need to release. There are people you have been attached to for too long. There are places you have been attached to for too long, and these things have held you hostage for way too long. They prevent you from moving forward and cause you many setbacks; you may be unaware of it, but it could be why you have not moved forward. Even though it is a comfortable place for you, you cannot imagine not having access to these things anymore because you were unintentionally feeding off their supply.

You have to be careful about carrying the orphan spirit, which causes you to need validation from people, things, and places, but understand that no matter what people say, you must seek validation from Christ. He is the true validator. He equips and validates you. You must be willing to untie yourself so you can experience God's freedom. There are people who speak words of affirmation into your life, but their hearts do not line up with what they say. They are content to offer insight and advice until you outperform them, and they secretly hope that the words they speak over your life do not come true. As you walk with God, you will discover who they are. However, you are comfortable with the person, and that keeps you attached.

When I was pregnant with my purpose, I began to mature in the things of God. I had to be honest with myself and remove myself from many relationships, noisiness, gossip, and leaches. It was not that I did not like them. I knew this season in my life did not include them. I could not be worried about what they thought; I had to do whatever it took to birth my purpose in a healthy state. You have to watch for people you are connected to who are spiritually sick.

Now let me set the record straight: No one is perfect. However, you should aim for perfection in all you do. I tell you to be careful of those who are unwell spiritually because it can be contagious. And without the right diagnosis or treatment, it could spread to you. You must relinquish these relationships. I have had people in my life I thought were for me. Every conversation started with, "How are you?" but after that, it was all about them and their situation. Be careful. They will suck the life out of you, leaving you empty and looking to be replenished. The Bible says iron sharpens iron. I suggest that as you seek to connect with others, make sure you are connecting with people you can sharpen and who can sharpen you. Proverbs 27:17 says, "Iron sharpens iron, and one man sharpens the face of His neighbor." There is a mutual benefit to speaking into the lives of others and causing them to become better through followership, leadership, friendship, and mentorship. This simple statement has been a call for all these years to understand that no one is alone.

In order to make yourself better, there is a mutual benefit of helping others through mentorship, followership, and leading. It is designed with love. It is positive even when there is a correction. Outside of people, places, and things, after breaking and relinquishing those soul ties you have adopted, you begin looking at what you are feeding yourself. Are you feeding yourself the Word of God, or are you feeding your body garbage but expect healthy results?

When a woman is pregnant with a child, there are things she should stop doing. If she drinks alcohol, she has to stop drinking it. If she smokes cigarettes or does drugs, she needs to stop because it increases the chance of a miscarriage or birth defects. A mother has to determine if she wants a healthy baby. It is the same for you. As you think about labor and delivery, let us discuss the things that you allow, specifically feeding your body and expecting healthy results. You allow space for the consumption of gossip or unhealthy music, and the foods, drinks, and toxins you allow your body to take in. You have to digest the fact "that your body is the temple of the Holy Spirit, who is in you, whom you have received from God, and that you are not your own" (1 Corinthians 6:19–20). You were bought at a price. It is important that you learn to let go of the things that do not line up with God's Word. These are things I began to make a consistent part of my life when I decided to choose God's way instead of my own.

You must pray. Prayer is our time to converse with God. He wants to talk with you, and it is so important that you establish a personal and intimate relationship with Him. He made you and loves you. God has the power to accomplish miracles, signs, and wonders in our hearts, and He can align your life with His vision and plan via prayer. That is why you are reading this book, which will help you learn how to pursue and acknowledge God's plan for your life so it might be fulfilled on earth. Paul reminds you of God's unending love and blessing for you. He connected the thought of praying without ceasing as an expression of appreciation and thankfulness to the Lord. You should "pray without ceasing," and Paul said it best: "We should give thanks in everything because this is the will of God in Christ Jesus pertaining to you." Pray without ceasing, and God will begin to download instruction and direction.

You must fast. A balanced diet is always good for you. Follow a healthy diet throughout this journey. Choose a healthy diet; it aids in maintaining a clear mind. "What? Do you realize that your body is the temple of the Holy Spirit, who lives within you and has been given to you by God, and that you are not your own? You were purchased at a cost. As a result, honor God in your body and spirit, which are both God's" (1 Corinthians 6:19–20). Fasting is something Jesus requires of His disciples. God is a rewarder of fasting. Fasting aids in the development of spiritual power, self-mastery, the development of your spiritual self, and the management of your body; it also helps you resist temptation. It will give you the strength to go through it because it is moving so quickly.

You must listen to Holy Spirit. When you listen to the Holy Spirit, you understand God's ways and the plan He has for you. You have to be sensitive to God's presence. The presence of God is encased in the triune God. The Holy Spirit is the third member of the Holy Trinity and is God's constant presence on earth. By residing in believers, the Holy Spirit qualifies them as Christians, allowing them to live a blameless and authentic life. The Holy Spirit is a comforter and also acts as an intercessor. The Holy Spirit also serves as a paraclete, someone who intercedes, encourages, assists, or represents as an advocate, especially in difficult circumstances. Stay connected and listen to the Spirit.

I could go on and on about what takes place as you release the things that have you bound. However, I would never finish the book. While going through this process, and as you continue on the journey, you must be willing to identify with the issues that paralyzed you. You must first be honest with yourself. If you are not honest with yourself, you will miscarry or experience defects at the time of birth. You must understand the assignment, which is to be free from the broken and fragmented pieces of your life. Once you identify who, what, when, and how, you must forgive so that God can forgive you.

Chapter Summary/Key Takeaways

Take time to reflect on where God ranks in your life. If He is not number one, you need to revisit what is taking His place. Having a healthy relationship with God is a priority. You will never discover who you are until you understand who He is. He created you for something greater than yourself. He made you in order for you to recognize and walk in our purpose, so that we can be a light to others in the same way that He was a light to you.

You must pray. This is your communication with God. Philippians 4:5–7 says, "Let everyone come to know your gentleness. The Lord is at hand. Be anxious for nothing, but in everything, by prayer and supplication with gratitude, make your requests known to God. And the peace of God, which surpasses all understanding, will protect your hearts and minds through Christ Jesus."

You should fast. Fasting aids in the development of self-control and discipline. Matthew 6:16–18 says, "Moreover, when you fast, do not be like the hypocrites with a sad countenance. Because they disfigure their faces, it may appear to men that they are fasting. Truly, I say to you, they have their reward. But you, when you fast, anoint your head and wash your face, so that you will not appear to men to be fasting, but to your Father who is in secret. And your Father who sees in secret, will reward you openly."

Listen to the Holy Spirit. Discerning the leading of the Holy Spirit is vital to living a Christian life. John 16:13 says, "But when the Spirit of Truth comes, He will guide you into all truth. For He will not speak on His own authority. But He will speak whatever He hears, and He will tell you things that are to come."

Chapter 6 discusses what happens when you carry the promises of God. It gives you a view of what the process may look like as you continue to move closer to the labor and delivery room. There are things that you will endure. There will be times when you will be stretched and feel uncomfortable, inconvenienced, and troubled. We discussed how you will have to be focused, tenacious, and determined to nurture God's promise. However, the next chapter will guide you through what is needed when preparing to birth your purpose. God's promise is so much bigger than the pushing, the pain, the loss, the loneliness, and the rejection you will experience. When you carry your purpose, you must protect it.

Prayer Is the Key: Not Looking Back Again

God the Father, I come before you, Father God, in the name of Jesus. Right where I am standing, right where I am crying, right where and when I want to go back and hold on to broken things. I surrender myself, my existence and mind, my hearing, what I see, what I am tied to, my anxieties, all attachments, pain, hurt, those uncomfortable places, humiliation, embarrassing situations, and the desire to return to or stay in the area of brokenness to you, Lord.

When my past confronts me and lurks, hovering and causing pressure, it pushes me into the dark recesses of my soul, attempting to compromise my thinking, where my grief, hurt, and embarrassment suffocate me. Destroy, pull down, remove, and set fire to the things that hover over me, preventing me from moving. Lord, I will no longer be inactive, missing out on your promise. I beg you to give me strength and stability. As I seek your face, I pray you will grant me guidance. I give myself over to you, God.

When the days come that I have an urge to go back to what is comfortable, allow Luke 10:19 to remind me that "I give you authority to trample on serpents and scorpions and over all the power of the enemy. And nothing will harm you in any way." Lord, I am thankful that your Word reminds me that you have given me the authority to trample on serpents and scorpions and over all the power of the enemy. And nothing shall by any means hurt me, in Jesus's name.

Lord, I ask that you fix the aspects of my life that are broken, and I freely commit my entire existence to you. I cannot accomplish anything without you, and without you, I am nothing. I do not want to be like Lot's wife; I want what you desire for me, God. I announce that today is my flesh day, and I submit to you, Lord. In the name of Jesus.

CHAPTER 6

CARRYING YOUR PURPOSE

Trust in the Lord with all your heart and lean not
on your own understanding. Acknowledge Him
in all your ways, and He will direct your paths.
—Proverbs 3:5–6

Many people talk about the desire to see miracles, signs, and wonders. However, we must do what it takes to see miracles, signs, and wonders manifest. We pray and fast for the blessings and promises of God and have a desire to see the Lord's favor rest upon our lives. However, when you carry the promises of God, you will have to go through some stuff. God will stretch you in uncomfortable, inconvenienced, and troubled times. You will have to be focused, tenacious, and determined to nurture God's promise. The time has come to give birth.

The process is needed when you are preparing to birth your purpose. God's promise is so much bigger than the pushing, the pain, the loss, the loneliness, and the rejection you will experience. You must stay focused during this stage of your journey because the journey can be a life-altering experience and should not be taken lightly. You must understand the preparation for birthing your purpose. There will be many transitions that will cause you to be uncomfortable. The more you grow, the heavier the weight becomes. However, the heaviness of the weight will be lifted at the appointed time. You have to put in the work. "Whatever a man sows, which shall also reap," says Galatians 6:7. Therefore, if you put in the work, you will see the manifestation of God's promise in your life.

For our sins, Jesus had to go through the process of coming to earth and dying on the cross. God was bruised; He was beaten; and He suffered just for us to be redeemed, delivered, and set free. I can only imagine the pain He endured. Think about it: Here we have Christ on the cross, dying, and while they do not believe He is the Messiah, Jesus is hanging there so that they might have life. Jesus did not want to do it, but He had to do it. It was His purpose and assignment. Whew. Could you imagine having the responsibility of dying for the sins of others? How about the fact that Jesus had to carry the weight of the world? He is a perfect God and had done nothing wrong. You must fulfill your purpose and assignment on this earth for similar reasons. There are many people attached to the call in your life. If you do not go through the process of carrying your promise to complete the assignments God has given you, many people may be lost. You are on this earth to walk in your God-given purpose with the mind of bringing light to someone else's darkness.

> To meet destiny, you must first birth purpose.
> ~Daphne Jett

Be reminded that the Lord entrusts you with these gifts and the call on your life. That is why you must discover your true identity to find out who you are and Who God is so He may reveal His plan for your life. God gives you the tools you need to nurture the gifts He has given you. Your gifts make room for you. You have to decide not to avoid the gift but to nurture it so it grows. You must carry its weight so you are strong enough to birth what He has put inside you. There is no way around it. You need to put in the work, but you must put in the work. However, you have to be careful about mishandling what God has given you. You must seek Christ to understand your God-given gift. What did He put you on this earth to complete? In my experience of counseling and speaking into the lives of others, I hear people tell me what they believe their gift is, and they are giving themselves titles and putting themselves in positions and roles God never assigned them to. Therefore, they are out of alignment. People are willing to sacrifice their God-given purpose to carry a title, just to be seen, or to feel a sense of acceptance, but they are not walking in what God has put them here on earth for. We cannot afford to waste time because the lives of God's sons and daughters depend on you walking in your God-given purpose. Some people are in the choir, and the praise and worship team should be ushers. Some people are ushers who should be ministers. Some people are out of alignment regarding what they should be doing. Now it is okay to help and serve in other areas of the church. Do not lose sight of the fact that you are responsible for pursuing your God-given purpose, even while serving.

God decides the gift He gives to His sons and His daughters. You do not get to choose. Therefore, it can be challenging because you never seem to get what you want. You do not determine what you carry. He equips you with what you need to complete the assignment. When a woman is pregnant, it does not matter if she wants a girl or a boy. You do not get to decide if you will birth a girl or a boy; God is the deciding factor. He knew us even before we were in our mothers' wombs and set us apart, so He already knew what we were going to be, even before we were formed. We do not get to choose. He chooses according to His plan and His purpose on earth. However, there will be times when it will take instructions and assistance from others God has ordained for your life.

When carrying your purpose and promise, make sure you have an inner circle you can count on to help assist you, guide you, support you, and challenge you in various areas. Make sure you have friends who understand the gift and the call and the weight of what you carry because they will hold you accountable. As Steve Marabella said, "Your greatest self has been waiting your whole life; don't make it wait any longer." Get with people who are moving in the direction you want to go. Chapter 4 talked about what it means to invest in yourself, so you must never stop educating yourself, through reading, seminars, conferences, events, and other avenues. I will repeat this. It is going to cost you something.

There are times when you have to spend money. Many people desire or want to be better. However, they do not want to invest financially if a financial investment is needed. Gautama Buddha said, "Those who have failed to work toward the truth have missed the purpose of living." No excuses, just forward movement. Being pregnant with the promise and going through the process will not be easy. You have to put in the work. There are times when you will lack the support of others. There are times when the wait appears to be unbearable. There are times when you will feel as though all the odds are against you while trying to accomplish the will of God for your life. Know that God sees you. He knows every difficulty that occurs as you carry and birth the promise, He has given you. The good thing about God is that He will never leave you nor forsake you. You must learn how to balance the weight of what you carry, even when it seems unbearable.

The Weight of What You Carry

As you continue to carry your purpose, there are so many things happening internally. This thing is growing inside of you, causing discomfort. At this point, you realize there are some things you cannot do because what you are carrying has grown too large for you to move the way you used to. There are times when it is hard to sleep because the position you used to sleep in is no longer comfortable. Because of the discomfort all you can think about is birthing a purpose. There is fluttering and kicking on the inside. You have gained momentum. You realize you are maturing mentally and spiritually. You begin to gain momentum through your consistency in reading, praying, fasting, and spending time with God. The more you feed your spirit, the closer you grow to Christ. The more confident you become the greater the momentum in pursuing your purpose. As you get closer, God starts downloading information to you through the Holy Spirit. God is preparing you for the birth by giving you instructions. The weight of what you are about to birth carries a price. You are so close to birthing your purpose. You are ready to get it out because you have been carrying it for too long. How will you know when the time comes? Do not give up, and do not give in.

While you continue on your journey, be mindful of what you say during this time. Remember, you have to be careful about what comes out of your mouth. You know, your words can produce what you speak, and the closer you get to seeing the promise of God, the more you become a severe threat to the enemy, and we know that he comes to kill, steal, and destroy. He comes to distort, he comes to distract, so we have to be aware of the risk as we go through the final stages of the process. Why? Because the enemy is going to try everything, he to get you to abort the promise of God. This is when you want to make sure you have on the full armor of God. Yes, we should wear it at all times. However, if at no other time, it is during this time because you are so busy preparing for your new life. This is the life that makes room for you, but first you have to prepare the room for it. Therefore, the enemy will come to strike, and this is why we must be clothed with the full armor of God. Ephesians 6:10–12 informs us that we should "be strong in the Lord and in the power of His might." Put on the whole armor of God so that you may be able to stand against the schemes of the devil. Ephesians 6:11 says, "For our fight is not against flesh and blood, but against principalities, against powers, against the rulers of the darkness of this world and against spiritual forces of evil in the heavenly places."

"Therefore, take up the whole armor of God so that you may be able to resist in the evil day, and, having done all, to stand. Stand therefore, having your waist girded with truth, having put on the breastplate of righteousness, having your feet fitted with the readiness of the gospel of peace, and above all, taking the shield of faith, with which you will be able to extinguish all the fiery arrows of the evil one. Take the helmet of salvation and the sword of the Spirit, which is the word of God. Pray in the Spirit always with all kinds of prayer and supplication. To that end, be alert with all perseverance and supplication for all the saints" (Ephesians 6:14–18).

We must be rooted in the Word of God. Remember, the Word is God. As a result, when we speak of scripture, we are speaking of God. When Jesus was tempted in the wilderness, He spoke the word of His Father. We must be able to speak God's Word in the midst of the enemy's tactics. We have to continue to read and meditate on God's Word day and night. Keep an eye out for the enemy's strategy and tricks as you carry out the promise. Because his plan is to make you believe you are not going to make it and you are not equipped to carry the promise to term. The enemy will send his angels to tell you things like you are not good enough, when in reality, you are more than enough. You are better than good. He will begin to bring up your past and try to get you to go back to those dark places in your life, but you have been renewed, restored, rejuvenated, and delivered.

You must know that you have been called to be the light, so you are a reflection of God. Your image was created in Christ. Continue to seek Christ during this time because there is a promise that will soon manifest.

The enemy wants to gaslight you by applying a weight that makes you feel like it is not worth it. He wants to kill your promise. He wants you to go back to an idle place where there is no movement.

You may begin to close yourself off from other people, and it is not healthy, so be careful as you carry your purpose to term. Know that there will be trials and tribulations that come. There may be turbulence. However, you have to be strong enough to deal with it and use God's Word. You have to make sure you have on the full armor of God and are ready for battle. Whatever it may cost you, you must ensure that you protect the gift. You have to be ready for the naysayers, the haters, and the people who speak positive words to you, but inside, they are praying against you. You have to be ready for those who truly do not want you to birth that which God has put inside you. People are going to say and do things to take you off course and distract you from moving forward. However, this birth must take place, and you want to make sure you are prepared. You are ready to push at the appointed time.

When God speaks the word, you are prepared to birth your purpose and are equipped to go forth, making sure God gets the glory. As you carry your purpose, be careful and tread lightly about where you go and what you do; be careful because there are risks. There is the possibility that you could stumble into the enemy's trap. When a woman is pregnant with a baby, there are certain things the doctor tells her she cannot do anymore. As she carries her baby, she has to be careful about holding her hands over her head, doing strenuous workouts, and so many other restrictions.

There are certain things outside of the nurturing process that you can no longer do as you birth your gift. The birthing season is soon to be upon you. While you go through this process, you have to be careful of the places you go. Remember, you are the light and no longer dwell in the dark places of your past. Therefore, do not allow people, places, or things to dim your light. Use wisdom and discernment in all you do and how you move, where you go, what you talk about, what you allow in your heart, and what you speak out of your mouth. It is out of the mouth that the heart speaks.

There are so many challenges that you face as you carry your purpose. It is imperative that as you go through the journey, you speak life to your purpose. It is also imperative that you carry the vision God has given you concerning that which He has called you to do on earth. The enemy may come to kill the promise you carry, but you must speak life and stay the course with the Word of God. Remember that no weapon formed against you will prosper. It may take form, but it will not prosper. That is the Word of the Lord.

My husband Kevin is very particular about our yard. When spring comes, there are so many weeds. He always plucks the weeds and cleans out the dead perennials from last year before the new ones begin to bud. One of the things I learned from him was that before you plant or before spring arrives and the new buds from your perennials begin reproducing, you have to pluck the weeds, and you cannot just pluck the weeds at the surface; you have to go deep. You have to get down low and pluck the weed at the root. If you do not pluck the weed at the root, it does not matter what you plant. You can plant the prettiest flowers you want, and you can be sure that the rain will come. Even when the perennials have broken the soil, the weeds will come back even stronger and have the potential to choke out the plant.

What I am saying to you is to be careful about the season you are in. Speak life to your purpose until you see the manifestation of it, because when you begin to confess words of affirmation over yourself, the enemy will come like a thief in the night, looking to take out anything that could assist you and fulfill your purpose. You must get to the root of every situation in your life that has hindered you. You must stay connected to the Holy Spirit and continue to read the Word of God as you move through this process. It will take God's words to get you through this journey. I want to reassure you that the turbulence will come to try and shake your foundation. You must stand on the promise and Word of God. There will be family, friends, and others who do not believe in you. They do not understand the call on your life, and they do not understand the priority of the call. They do not understand the people who are attached to the call. They do not understand the significance of your call, and they are really not interested because they are too busy looking at your past. They are too busy identifying you for what they know about you. They are too busy passing judgment on you based on their perception of you.

The unfortunate part is that the very people who speak against you do not realize they were supposed to be connected to you, but they allowed the enemy to distort their vision and see you in a dysfunctional way. That is why they are not walking in what is designed for them. Stay on course with the things of God. You must think bigger. You must speak the truth. Continue to move. You know God has changed you. He has reconditioned your mind. You see life differently because you know your true identity in Christ. The critics and your faultfinders are still stuck in your past. You cannot carry this along with you. You cannot allow other people's issues to take precedence over what the Word of the Lord says, or it will set you back. It could cause you to miss the promise of God. Some things will come up against you, but you have to stay strong.

Connect with people who will help you nourish your gift so you walk in boldness as you go forth, knowing who you are and what you possess inside. We will discuss this in Chapter 9. As you experience the weight of what you carry, there will come a time in the process when God releases you from these weights. That happened in the delivery room. You have to protect and guard what you carry. Being in the wrong place with the wrong people at the wrong time can cause you to go into premature labor. It can cause you to abort the promise. It can cause you to miscarry and never see the promises of God fulfilled in your life.

This is why it is so important that you are connecting with the right people. These are the people who truly speak words of affirmation to you when you are unable to affirm yourself. As you continue to go through the process, you want to be connected with people who understand that what you carry is a gift from God. They understand that what you carry is bigger than what you yourself understand or can comprehend and that what you carry will bring life not just to you, but to those who need to hear from you. They need your purpose to be activated; they need you to move forward in it so they can move in the things of God and fulfill the plan for their lives. You must be in your rightful place as it pertains to the call on your life because there are people who need to be touched by the Word of God that flows from you. It is vital that you walk out the call of God on your life and that you are as bold as a lion.

I had a coworker who was a people-pleaser. It did not matter what the situation was, she wanted to ensure that everyone was in favor of her decisions. The reality was that she was not happy. There were times she would hear things people said about her, and anytime she was around that person, she would try to please them. When she was in their presence, she would try to make sure that what she heard was not what they saw when they were around them. The goal was to change their perception of her. She knew that what they perceived of her was not true. She knew that was not who she was.

One day, during a conversation, my coworker shared her experience with the departments with which she works on a daily basis. She shared the perception people on the job had about her and who started the rumors. One of the things I told her is that not everyone will like you.

People will accept the opinions of others before getting to know you for themselves and forming their own opinions. Psalm 110:1 tells us, "People that do this seem not to be able to think for themselves." You have to know who you are because many times, people will say things that are not true. I proceeded to tell her that people will say things about you to make themselves feel better about themselves. I shared with her that the Lord is faithful, and He is just. He will make your enemies your footstool. She had to learn who she was in Christ, and it would not come easily, and it did not come overnight. She had to shift her mindset from a negative to a positive. It did not matter what they thought, she had to focus on what God thought about her. People will fail, but God will never fail. I shared with her that "as a man thinketh, so is he" (Proverbs 23:7).

Therefore, if you think negatively, you will get negative results, but if you think positively, you will begin to see positivity manifest in your life. We have to learn not to sweat the small things in life. Carrying the weight of what someone thinks about you is not your problem. Pray for them, give it to God, and keep moving. God will reveal many things to you pertaining to people and the direction of your life. You have to be willing to listen and not rebuke the Word of the Lord because it is not what you want to hear. God is like any other parent; He corrects you when you are out of alignment and not obedient. He will never leave you or forsake you, so you are never alone. Trust Him.

So, as you carry your purpose to term, make sure you are mindful of the people around you. I am talking about people you have been friends with for years; they do not want to see you move forward. They pretend they do, but they really do not. These people say they will pray for you, and the reality is that they are not praying for you. As a matter of fact, have you ever seen them pray? God connects you with people who are mature enough to handle what He has sent and called you to do at the right time. Not everyone can handle it. You are growing in your purpose. Many times, they cannot handle it because they have not yet taken the steps and gone through the process themselves.

People will be okay with your growth as long as you are on the same playing field as them. As long as you are one step behind them, gossiping with them and talking about people, when you get to a place where that is no longer your conversation. This can cause you to lose friends. The reality is that you are maturing in the call God has ordained for you. They are not a part of this season in your life. You must be connected to it in order to see it come to pass. You realize that you recognize the weight of what you are carrying. There are things you will have to sacrifice. You have to mature in the things of God. 1 Peter 2:2 says, "As newborn babies, desire the pure milk of the word, that by it you may grow." 1 Corinthians 3:2–3 says, "I have fed you with milk and not with solid food. To this day, you are not able to endure it. Nor are you able now, for you are still worldly. Since there is envy, strife, and divisions among you, aren't you worldly and behaving like mere men?"

Let me say it before you do. I know you are not perfect, but you should be aiming for perfection. There is a time when God wants to see maturity in his people. This is when you ask God to give you understanding about maturing in Him so you may carry this thing with dignity, character, integrity, and the Lord's protection. That is why you must not share what you have with everyone. Be careful. You have to be able to determine who you should be sharing with. As you carry the promise, do not allow yourself to adopt the orphan spirit that runs rampant in the insecure. The orphan spirit is when you need validation from others. Validation can be a risk to carrying your purpose if it is not someone you are supposed to be connected to in this period of your life. It can take you off course; it can make you have premature labor pains, so be mindful of what you receive from other people.

Carrying your purpose is also a time where you are uncomfortable. Think about how a woman's baby begins to grow to a certain size, month by month. There are certain ways she can sleep. She can no longer sleep on her stomach, and she has to readjust. It can be uncomfortable because she has to change her position from the way she usually sleeps. There is morning sickness. There are things she can and cannot eat that cause her to regurgitate, and when those things happen, she has to rethink what she needs to do to become more comfortable.

I can remember being in high school and carrying my bookbag on my shoulder. There were times when the books were so heavy that my arm hurt from carrying the bag. After I walked home from school, I felt like my arm was going numb because of the weight of the books in the bag. I had to readjust the books in my bag or figure out how to carry them so that I could balance the weight. Sometimes, you have to readjust the weight. Things become uncomfortable as they grow. You are aligning and have been obedient to listening to the Holy Spirit as you moved through this journey, and even though the labor pains have not yet come, your body is adjusting. Your discernment is stronger, and you have begun to believe the call on your life. What does the Word of the Lord say about you? You yearn to know Him more, so much so that you want to pray to Him and establish a relationship with Him. The Word of the Lord has become a part of your daily routine. Things happen as you carry your purpose. You see through a different lens now. Your desire gets bigger, and you gain insight into the discovery of your purpose.

You have nurtured this thing, so now its purpose has grown inside of you and makes you uncomfortable. The enemy wants to distort you vision and make you lose focus. Stray focused on the task at hand and carry out your purpose. If you feel it is too heavy or you are about to give out, keep moving. I know it feels as though you have no more room to grow, and your purpose has become weighty. I know you feel like you cannot take on anything else. Keep momentum. You have heard the saying, "No pain, no gain," and when you get to this place of discomfort, readjust yourself and do not lose momentum. Do not lose sight of the value of what you carry.

The Word of the Lord says we shall reap the harvest if we faint not. You have to remember you are feeding it what thus saith the Lord, so you are carrying your purpose, and all these things are happening. When a mother becomes a certain size, she can no longer fit into the clothes she wore before she was pregnant. She must buy things that fit her current size. So be mindful of the stage that you are currently in. From a birthing standpoint, there are growing pains that prepare you for what is next. Although the weight of what you carry can be overwhelming, you must focus. Do not lose sight of the promise. Your birthing season has not yet arrived, but it is soon to come. You are now stepping into a maturity that you have never experienced before.

These things either slow down or completely stop the flow of movement in a person's life, which prevents them from fulfilling the call on their life. I am here to tell you that you are deserving, that you are more than enough, and that you deserve every prophecy and promise that God has spoken over your life. You must go after him and make a move. You move, and in your obedience, your rump smacks dead into purpose and destiny concerning the call on your life. The more you learn about God, the more He will reveal to you His plan for your life. Make sure you do not allow your insecurities, your past, or your thoughts to convince you that you are not enough to fulfill the plan of God. I have seen where not relinquishing these issues has caused spiritual blood clots in the minds and hearts of God's sons and daughters.

Chapter Summary/Key Takeaways

When you carry your purpose, you must be mindful of what you carry because it is valuable. You have to make sure you protect the gift. You are so close to delivery.

1. The process is needed when you are preparing to birth your purpose.
2. You are held accountable to fulfill God's plan.
3. You have to change your mindset. You can no longer think the same way.

Chapter 7 gives insight into what your support system should look like. It gives guidance on who your support system should be, how to ensure you have the right people supporting you, and what to take with you. It is a time to prepare for the overnight stay during the time of travail.

Prayer Is the Key: Relief from Anxiousness

Lord Jesus, it appears that the tensions in my life frequently reach deadly proportions. My body, mind, and spirit are all struggling to keep up on a physical, mental, and spiritual level. Anxiety hunts me like a cunning predator on some days, and the desire to worry lures me in. Help me remember that I belong to You and that You are not the cause of fear or anxiety, but rather the giver of love and a sound mind in those moments of apprehension. Teach me how to respond to problems by thanking God for them. Your Word informs me that You are with me at all times. You are the Blessed Controller of all things, and nothing escapes Your attention in my life. You have given me every tool and spiritual blessing to fight against those things that try to steal my peace. You have promised that when I am stressed, and burdens are trying to weigh me down, I can come to You. You will give me a sweet rest.

Lord, forgive me for attempting to handle things on my own. At times, the need to be in charge of my life has a grasp on me. That only makes things worse. I want to trust You more and see things from Your perspective, not my own. No one makes me feel anxious, angry, or stressed, and no one forces me to react negatively. I choose to respond according to my beliefs. When an anxious thought creeps in, help me stop, relax, take that thought captive, and turn apprehension into a calm prayer for deliverance.

Lord, help me to rethink my beliefs. Show me a new method to deal with life in Your way. I am leaving them all at Your feet today. No matter what troubles I am dealing with, and no matter how serious the problems or situations are, I am leaving them all at Your feet today. Turn these stressors into opportunities for growth and trust. When I do not see any other options, I choose to trust that You are working things out for my good in Your own time, as You have done in the past. Please show me how to do something or how not to do something. I believe You will fill me with a serenity beyond all understanding as I focus on You, remembering Your promises and words. Amen.

CHAPTER 7

PREPARING FOR THE STAY

But He said to me, "My grace is sufficient for you,
for *My* strength is made perfect in weakness."
Therefore, most gladly I will boast in my weaknesses,
that the power of Christ may rest upon me.
—2 Corinthians 12:9

The day is almost here. You are waiting for the day to arrive at this point. However, preparation is essential. Before the labor pains come, you should make sure you have prepared a bag for labor, delivery, and recovery. Prepare a bag as soon as possible because you will not be able to prepare for labor and delivery once the labor pains come. When you get to a place where you feel as though you are fighting the pain and the pain becomes unbearable, make sure you have packed your overnight bags because the labor pain is soon to begin.

When a woman prepares her bag, she puts so many items in it. There are clothes and things for the baby and mom to wear home, as well as Mom's personal items. The mother ensures she has everything she needs in her bag for her stay. Also, she ensures that she has designated the person responsible for getting her safely to the hospital and the one who knows where she placed her overnight bag. When the labor pain starts, whoever she has put in control of her hospital bag knows where it is and can locate it. In addition

> What you carry is valuable to God. Make sure who you around can be trusted!
> ~Daphne Jett

to the overnight bag, the mother creates a call list of those important to her. She gives the person responsible for the overnight bag instructions on who to call and the priority they should give each person. The mother also lets the person know the location of the list in the bag. Who are these people, and why are they on this call list? These are the people the mother will provide access to during different stages of her stay. These are the people in your life who carry a high level of importance. You are about to give birth to a valuable gift, so you want to ensure that the people who hold esteem and value in your life are there. This list is your support system.

What you carry is valuable to God. Therefore, you have to ensure you have a support system that can be trusted. You must understand the weight of what you carry. This time is sacred, not to mention that what you are about to give birth to has the anointing of God. Your purpose is being birthed into the earth not only so you fulfill God's plan for you, but also so God can be glorified in everything you do in accordance with the assignments He gives you. Your purpose is to give life to others. Not everyone understands or believes in what you possess. Not everyone can see how much you had to travail. They are not privy to that information. God allows some people connected to you to know that you have a purpose, but not all know the magnitude.

Some people will be upset because they did not know you were in labor. It is not that you do not care about them; you just need to protect the gift. Protecting the gift means you are careful about the people you give access to at this moment. You will find that people say one thing out of their mouths, but their hearts and mouths are not aligned. You have to know that when the labor pains come, the pressure will make you feel as though you are being crushed, and the enemy will show up at that moment to tell you that you will never birth what is inside of you because you are not strong enough. Therefore, you must ensure that the people on your call list are ready to go to battle for you and are willing to carry the weight when you go into labor. The enemy will come, so seek God as you prepare your list, and be honest with yourself first. You cannot have the faint-of-heart with you at this time. You have to have people surrounding you who will not faint when you push! You must make sure they do not faint when the birth occurs.

You must have warriors on the battlefield who are willing to fight and bear the burdens of your pain in order for them to be strong in the Lord's Word. Prepare for battle and prepare for the enemy's tactics. They must be able to stand firm on the Word of the Lord, so that even when the wind and the pain come, even when the squeezing and the crushing come, they can stand in the gap for you. I am here to tell you, not everyone belongs on the list. If you have to contemplate or question whether they should be on the list, cross them out quickly because they will not make the cut. During the time of pain, it is time to fight. You must call in the King David's, who are strategic in their approach and have planned out how to slay a giant, no matter how big; not just slay the giants in their way, but for you too. The enemy does not want you to fulfill your God-given purpose. The enemy does not want to see the prophecy of God manifest in your life. I suggest that you pray and ask God who to connect with in this birthing season.

The Call List

The call list is significant. We discussed that you have to be careful about who you are connected to in this birthing season. Some people we call friends are not true friends. They are acquaintances. Many times, the word "friend" is used without thought. The word does not have much meaning for many people. Therefore, be sure not to mix acquaintances with friends when birthing your purpose. You have to use discernment to determine who truly deserves to be a part of your life. The first two on the list are your immediate family and best friend. They are there to celebrate the birth of a new family member. They are in the waiting room with anticipation, waiting to celebrate the birth of a new life and a new addition to the family. Our immediate family does not have access to the delivery room until after the birth. Once they obtain access, only a specific number of family members can come in at a time.

Second, you want to make sure your support system is on the list. These people are usually in the waiting room with the family, but they understand your journey to get to this point. Your support system understands the pressures, turbulence, pain, and weight you have experienced through this process. They are the ones who not only sit in the waiting room and wait for the birth to celebrate, but they are there to fill in the gaps and be in a place of prayer. They are praying for healthy birthing, strength, and endurance because they understand what you endure to get to this place of delivery. They are prayer warriors. Your support system is not just there for the excitement. They are there to pray for continued strength as you go from the labor room into delivery and recovery. Be careful. Be incredibly careful not to allow just anyone to be your support system. Remember, your support system is not allowed further than the waiting room. The prayer warriors are only there as support to see you through the birthing process through prayer.

Third, you want to ensure that your midwife is on the list. Your spiritual midwife is responsible for nursing the progress of your pregnancy and preparing you for delivery. The midwife's focus is on labor, delivery, and recovery, and she must be a part of your labor and delivery experience. The midwife helps you nurture the gift after the birth. She must have access to the labor and delivery room before and after the child's birth. The midwife is the nurturer, your pusher, and the one who gives instruction downloaded from the Holy Spirit. The midwife is connected to God and has been assigned to you to ensure that the birth comes forth as God designed and to assist in nurturing the gift. The midwife instructs you when to breathe and push during the birth. God gives her insight into the size and value of what you are birthing. She intercedes and receives downloads from the Holy Spirit because she has guided you and imparted in you throughout this process. She has been there for you in every phase, from conception to birth. Your midwife is connected, so she knows what to intercede for even when you are not around. She has been proactively talking to the Father on your behalf. The call on her life is to ensure that you walk out yours.

God has ordained and connected the midwife to your life. Do not take her for granted. You are a part of her assignment. The midwife understands the promise of God as it pertains to your life. She has had a glimpse of your gift and the call on your life. The midwife understands the capacity of what you are birthing. She is there to make sure you do not fold, but you follow through. You must understand the importance of the midwife and why God sends her. Only a few people can go into the labor and delivery room when the birthing begins. Not everyone deserves access. God should be the one to authorize them.

Your Spiritual Support Team

Having the support of those who understand what you are carrying has its benefits. They care for your well-being, encourage you when you feel deflated, pray when you need strength, ensure that you and the baby are well, and push your purpose when you want to give up. Your support system should assist with the reduction of anxiety, tension, and pressure. They are there to empower, inspire, and energize you when you are weak. During the preparation time, you must be intentional. The preparation time is the time to be focused. You cannot make decisions based on your emotions or the opinions of others. You must protect the gift while carrying it. Never forget that the enemy always seeks out those he can devour. Do not get too comfortable. I suggest you seek Christ and ask Him for guidance in your decisions as you go through the process.

This process is no different than a basketball game. A team has twelve players, but only five of them can be on the court during the game. There are substitutions when players on the court cannot play at their full potential, so they are removed from the game, and a substitute who is well-rested is brought in. This is how it is when we think about our walk with God. You have to know who your strongest players are. Who wants to see you win and provides you with what you need to make a winning shot? They understand that when you win, we all win, not to mention the Kingdom of God wins, as one body in Christ. You have to know when the players do not have the strength to get you to a win. It is not that you are getting rid of them; they have to sit out to regain their endurance and strength to beat their opponent.

You have to know who you should connect with in every season of your life. You have to be strategic and intentional in your decisions. Not everyone you talk to or see as a friend has your best interests at heart. I have encountered many people I have given access to my life, assuming they were for me because of what they spoke out of their mouths. I later found out that many of these people were not who I thought they were. These are the people who cannot go into the birthing room.

When you give birth to greatness, you must be confident that the people you bring with you will support you, and you must be willing to support them. I can remember traveling with one of my mentors. When I traveled to learn from her, I remember an event that we attended. The groups were paired together and given an assignment. The assignment was that we were to pray and wait for a download from the Holy Spirit about the person we partnered with. I began to share with her the information God had given me, and then she began to share what God had given her to say to me. They were definitely words ordained by God. It was confirmation for the two of us. She said one thing to me, and now and then, she still says it. It has changed my thought process regarding helping others become their best selves, personally, professionally, and in their walk with Christ.

She said, "You must understand that iron sharpens iron." You must connect with purpose partners who recognize your value of what you carry and they are willing to invest in you and push you.

When you seek the face of God, ask Him who the people you have been called to connect to in this season of your life are. God will give you revelation. There are times when He will place someone in your life solely for the purpose of your current season. They may fulfill a supporting role through the birthing process, so you must seek Him first. Make sure you are praying and studying His Word, and He will download information through the Holy Spirit. You must be willing to listen to Him.

Now that you are in the preparation stages and have prepared your bag with everything you need, you must "trust in the Lord with all of your heart and lean not on your own understanding. In all of your ways, you should acknowledge Him, and He will direct your path" (Proverbs 3:5–6).

Having a support system ensures you have a network of people who give emotional and practical support. Your support system will assist you through every stage of the process by helping you get through the uncomfortable and challenging times throughout this journey.

Chapter Summary/Key Takeaways

Make sure you have a support system that truly supports you. Ensure your support system is filled with the Word of God and ready for battle. They understand the gift you carry and are willing to be your support in and out of the birthing room.

1. When you give birth to greatness, you must be confident that the people you bring with you will support you, and you must be willing to support them.
2. Make sure you understand the role and responsibilities of the support system God has given you.

Chapter 8 reminds us of the expectations of growing spiritually. Spiritual maturity is something every Christian should strive for. It has a significant impact on how you serve God, engage with others, and care for your family. The next chapter delves into the many people who claim to be Christians, but there is a distinction to be made between being a fan of Jesus and being one of His followers. What side of the fence you are on, can be determined by where you in Christ spiritually. Being a disciple of Jesus requires you to deny yourself, take up your cross, and follow Him. When He called the people to Him with His disciples, He said to them, "If any man would come after Me, let him deny himself, take up His cross, and follow Me" (Mark 8:34).

CHAPTER 8

THE IMPORTANCE OF SPIRITUAL GROWTH

Brothers, do not be children in your thinking; rather
be infants in evil, but in your thinking be mature.
—1 Corinthians 14:20

Growing spiritually is vital for every believer. "Jesus called you to not only believe in Him but also to be His disciple" (James 2:19). Being a disciple of Christ is more than just knowing God exists. It is important that as you disciple, you should follow and reproduce the things you have learned through Christ and that it is done for His glory, based on truth, which is the Word of God. Hebrews 6:1 says, "Therefore, leaving the elementary principles of the doctrine of Christ, let you go on to maturity, not laying again a foundation of repentance from dead works and of faith toward God." You must move from a stagnant place, where you are not growing spiritually. Think about it: If you are a parent and do not feed your children throughout the day, they will starve over a period of time from malnutrition. This stunts their growth and could potentially cause serious health issues. It is the same for your spiritual life.

It is so important that there is spiritual growth happening amongst believers. It is critical that as you walk with Christ, you mature in Him and not just be churchgoers. Too many people are doing church but not following Christ. As long as you remain in a stagnant place, you will find that it will not bring any good to your life. As you grow spiritually, push yourself to spend time with God so you can move on to the things He tells you through the Holy Spirit, not what you believe but what God is saying.

As you go through the process of birthing the promise, God prepares you. If you study the truth, which is in the Word of God, you will realize you have confused the truth about spiritual growth. 1 Corinthians 14:33 tells us, "For God is not the author of confusion, but of peace, as in all churches of the saints." God is the author of peace. When it comes to looking for an understanding of spiritual growth, you must pursue the Word of God. You must pursue God's sacred scripture. There is no substitute or alternative way but to read the Word of God. Examine God's Word. You must grow in grace and in knowledge of our Lord and Savior, Jesus Christ. To Him be the glory, forever and ever. Amen.

2 Peter 3:18 defines spiritual growth in a simplistic manner. Spiritual growth is nothing more than growing in the grace and knowledge of our Lord and Savior, Jesus Christ. You must become immersed in the Word of God to be dedicated and disciplined and become students of the Word of God. It is not enough to just read the Word. You must become students of the Word because God is the Word. To know the Word is to know Him. Genesis 1:1–4 declares, "In the beginning was the Word, and the Word was with God, and the Word was God. He was in the beginning with God. All things were created through Him, and without Him nothing was created that was created. In Him was life, and the life was the light of mankind. "You must know Who created all existence and Who created us. By understanding and studying His Word, you grow spiritually.

When you become a student of the Word of God, you become conversant about the truth through the revealing from Holy Spirit. When I begin my studies of the Word of God, I pray to the Father, asking Him to open my heart and understanding as I partake in examining His Word. God will reveal His Word to you. Spiritual growth is nothing more than growing and maturing in your understanding and an intimate relationship with God.

We know that all living things are expected to grow. If it starts with a seed and is planted, the expectation

> You must become immersed in the Word of God to be dedicated and disciplined and become students of the Word of God.
> ~ Daphne Jett

is that it will produce. Whether it grows or not depends on the soil and the foundation that is being created. Think about yourself. When you were a baby, you crawled, learned to walk and learned to talk based on the environment you were in. You moved from a place of dependency on your parents to becoming an independent adult. So, there was a process to your independence. You did not just go from a baby to an adult without a process or journey. There are growth spurts that happened within the process. I can remember when my son was about ten years old, and he was about four feet tall. There was a growth spurt that happened because by the time he was thirteen, he was almost six feet tall.

Through every season of your life, there will be opportunities for you to grow spiritually. You have to make a choice to grow. However, you must seek after God because that is where you find peace, joy, hope, and love. As you are going through this process, there will be times that are uncomfortable for you. However, you cannot forget about God. Because as you go on into maturity, when you become independent, you may feel as though you do not need God anymore, and that you are in control of your life. You must come into the revelation of acknowledging your dependency on God and learning to trust Him instead of people. God will never fail. He will never leave you, and He will never forsake you. When you understand who He is and as you grow into maturity and establish a healthy relationship with Him, you will begin to understand how much you need the Father.

People say God wants His children to mature. At some point in the process, through the journey, during the growth spurts, God expects His children to mature. If you are not maturing in the things of God, if you are still a baby in Christ and have a desire to mature, you must go after His work. It has to become a part of your everyday living. I said it before, and I will say it again: You must read His Word, and most importantly, become a student of His Word. Then and only then will you run smack dead into maturity. It will sneak up on you before you realize how much you have grown.

God Is Preparing You for the Promise

I can only tell you from my experience that staying a baby in Christ and being dependent on other people did not benefit me, and as I aged, I had to understand just because I was aging with the years, it did not mean that I was maturing. I was getting older, but it was my mindset that needed to change in order to birth my purpose and experience God's promise. Therefore, I had to get to a place that I had to pursue, seek out, invest, dedicate time, and become a student of the Word of God so as I matured in His Word, He would shift my thoughts. Funny, when I look at my life now and see where I am from a maturity perspective, it amazes me. I am not perfect, but I am maturing and understanding His Word, learning His voice, and connecting with the Holy Spirit in a way that when God sends me out on an assignment, I have the ability to listen to the spirit of God.

There was a time in my life when I was not mature. There were many days I had to continuously readjust my thinking. Trust me, I got it wrong many times in my head and had to start over. It is not an easy shift, because to change your mindset, you have to think differently about who you are. There were many people in my life who caused me to see the opposite of what God created me to be. In my experience over the years, people have hurt me, lied to me, disappointed me, and even tried to destroy my character. I cannot lie; yes, it hurt. I did not want to forgive people for the hurt they caused me, even though I knew that in order for God to forgive me, I had to forgive them. The pain I allowed was at a time in my life when I was young. I did not know who I was.

As I became older, I still had not yet discovered me, so I carried the weight of my pain for many years, when I should have let it go a long time ago. I could only see myself in a distorted way. The enemy stole my sight and kept me from God's truth. Yes, the enemy sent his angels to disrupt, shut down, tear down, kill, steal, and destroy my life. He used people to cause me anguish, even when they did not know they were being used. Even though I carried the weight of other people's words, I knew I had to go through it. It was a part of the process. I also knew I had to go through it, because if I had not gone through it, I would not be the woman I am today. There will be pressure as you go through life and as you grow spiritually. Not all is from the enemy. God created you, called you, and ordained you. He knows exactly what it will take to get you to the place of birthing your promise and being able to execute from a healthy place. He knows what your physical, spiritual, and mental states must be in order for you to carry what He has placed within you.

It was not until I became completely sold out and disciplined in my walk with Christ that I realized He loved me. God's authentic, unwavering love is something you will have to experience on your own. No man, no woman, no pastor, no friend, no one can give you the encounter you experience with God like the one you experience through prayer, through studying God's Word, and through communing with the Holy Spirit. My life has been forever changed through this journey. The battle is never over. There will always be something that comes to throw you off course or make you feel inadequate. God's Word says, "Pay attention all Judah, and those dwelling in Jerusalem, and King Jehoshaphat: Thus says the Lord to you, 'Do not fear, nor be dismayed because of this great army, for the battle is not yours, but God's'" (2 Chronicles 20:15). What I will say is that you are in for the fight of your life. The process has to take place. Do not give up. I did not give up. I kept pressing because I knew there was something great growing inside me.

If a baby stays in the womb for too long, it causes risks to the health of the baby, which is why the doctor will often perform a C-section. There will come a time when your purpose is growing inside of you and there is no more room to grow. You will know when that time comes, because the pain you will experience from the stretching will be upon you. I have lived it. As God continues to plant, you will continue to birth the new. Prepare yourself for all He has for you.

You must move forward. Do not make excuses for why you have not started pursuing your purpose; instead, start thinking of all the reasons why you should. You are never too young or too old. You have to know when to pick up your mat and go forth. Walk. God has provided you with everything you need to complete the task He has given you. Even the lame man had to get up and walk when Peter told Him to get up. He came to a specific location every day with the same mindset: "Because I was born this way, because I have this defect, I will never be able to work." The lame man had a distorted mindset. He never thought to ask for healing. He was willing to stay in his brokenness and dysfunction and settle for the least.

However, Peter did not have what the lame man wanted. What Peter had, he gave, and that was the power of God through the Holy Spirit.

It is the same for you. Walk. Connect with people who are mature in their faith and their walk with God, who see what God sees in you. They understand what you carry. Most importantly, they are willing to support you to the end. Not to be nosy, or to gossip, but they are there to see you birth the gift you carry.

What It Means to Grow Spiritually

We hear a lot about growing spiritually, and to be honest, there are so many people who do not realize what that means. They think it is just going to church. They go to church on Sunday, they give an offering, they clap their hands to the worship songs, and they listen to the pastor for forty-five minutes, which requires them to open up their Bible to read the scriptures. There are times I have been in churches and ministries where the focus is on getting people into the church and getting people to pray, which is not a bad thing. However, there needs to be some post-decision care. What do I mean by that? There are times when new people come into a place of worship, and if you ask them if they are Christian, they are going to say yes. However, few of them understand what being a follower of Jesus Christ means. This is not a one-time decision; it is a day-after-day-after-day process of growth spiritually. This is biblical growth. You are to mature spiritually. Examine Hebrews 5:11–13: "Concerning this you have much to say that is hard to explain, since you have become hard of hearing. By now you should be teachers, you need someone to teach you again the first principles of the oracles of God and have come to need milk rather than solid food. Everyone who lives on milk is unskilled in the word of righteousness, for he is a baby." You must grow and not just sit by, idle.

I have heard so many people tell me it is not their time or season. It may not be your time or season, but prepare yourself so when your season comes, you are ready. Do not prepare when the season is upon you. You are to prepare before the season comes, so that you are ready to execute and fulfill the works of God. You have to get out of your own way. I hear so many excuses, like, "I am waiting on God." And my question is, what are you waiting for? If who He called, He equipped, then He has given you everything you need to move. You have his permission to move! 2 Thessalonians 3:10 says, "For when we were with you, we commanded you that if any will not work, neither shall he eat." As a result of not working or operating in accordance with your purpose, you are not seeing the promises of God. You are looking at others wanting to be in that place, but they have put in the work. You must get to work and begin operating according to your purpose. God has designated you to be a light in the lives of others, just as He is a light in ours.

It is time to get moving. It does not matter if someone is doing it; God made you unique, and there is more than enough room on earth for every gift from God to be used effectively. Proverbs 18:16 says, "A man's gift makes room for him and brings Him before great men."

The preparation stage comes before the harvest season. You must water and uproot the things in your life that do not reflect the image of God prior to the season. As you go through the process of awakening or unraveling your gift, identifying, discovering, investing, and preparing, you will experience growth spurts along the way, as long as you stay connected to the Holy Spirit through the Word of God. You will begin to realize at some point in the process how much you have grown. There are times when you do not see your growth until you become uncomfortable. We will discuss this in detail in Chapter 8. It is time to mature. Do not look at others who made it through the process and feel envious of them because it is what you desire for yourself. You must put in the work. I have learned that walking in maturity takes a shifting in your mind as it pertains to your personal and Christian life. Hebrews 5:14 reveals that "solid food belongs to those who are mature, for those who through practice have powers of discernment that are trained to distinguish good from evil." So, stay the course because birthing your purpose is scheduled for a set time. Continue to pray throughout the process, seeking God's face and those He has connected you to through this journey.

You Must Become Christlike

You must become more like Christ as you grow spiritually. Before I met Christ and realized who He was, I never considered spiritual growth and what it looked like through a spiritual lens. I was so caught up in my failures, my pain, and my disappointment that as I sought Christ, I never looked back to see how far I had come. You cannot go back to dead places, and you should not go back to dead places. However, there are times when God will allow you to catch a glimpse of the things you have been through so you can measure how far you have come and the things you have overcome. 2 Peter 1:3–8 reminds you that "by the power of God that rests inside you, you have everything you need to fulfill the plan of God concerning your life of godliness." Walking in the power of God that is in you is considered spiritual maturity.

When you get to the point that you recognize you have matured from where you were before in the process, you will continue to press forward as you endure the labor pains and the stretching. You will be able to make it past the pain, the roadblocks, and the trials that you previously could not survive. The reason is because you now wear the full armor of God, and the more mature you become in who you are and in Whose you are, the bolder you grow, and you begin to understand that you must birth what God has put inside you at all costs. Remember, it will cost you something. You must be ready to fight the good fight of faith, as you endure the journey in preparation of birthing the promise God planned for your life. When you get to a place where you are able to recognize that you have matured, you will be able to make it past the roadblocks and trials that you may experience along the way. I am not saying it will not hurt, but you will be able to withstand the pressure more than before. When the enemy comes to test you, he comes about like a roaring lion, seeking whom He may devour. You must resist Him using the Word of God as a shield. You must be steadfast in the faith (1 Peter 5:8–9).

Transformation and Growth

When the transformation of salvation takes place, spiritual growth begins. The Holy Spirit indwells us (John 14:16–17). You become a new creature in Christ (2 Corinthians 5:17). The old, sinful way of doing things begins to give way to the new things of becoming Christlike (Romans 6–7). Spiritual growth is a lengthy process, and it is contingent upon applying and studying God's Word. Remember to be a student of the Word of God. As you continue to walk through the process of birthing your promise, you will continue to grow spiritually. As you continue to grow spiritually, you must pray and ask God to give you wisdom in the areas where He wants you to grow. The Bible tells you that if you ask for wisdom, God will give it to you. You can ask God to increase your faith and your understanding of Him because He delights in you growing spiritually. He has equipped you with everything you need to grow spiritually. Make sure you stay connected to the Holy Spirit as you continue to grow.

The Holy Spirit is your assistant and your helper. He helps you to overcome sin and progressively become more like Christ. As you continue to grow and define areas where you need to grow, here are some key points to understanding when you are growing spiritually.

When you love something or someone, you chase after it. It makes no difference how much it costs, how far you have to reach, or how wide you have to stretch. When you love something, the desire causes you to do whatever it takes to get to that place, that person, or that thing. It needs to be the same with your desire and love for God. If you love God, then why don't you chase after Him? Why don't you pursue Him? If you do not build a relationship with God, and if you do not know His Word, you cannot connect with the Holy Spirit; therefore, you will never walk in your true identity. You must learn more about God so you can begin to mature in the things of God and not continue to sit stagnant in a place. God created you to have a servant's heart.

When you move into the things of God and begin to search and seek Him, when you are growing and maturing in Christ as a Christian, it is not enough to wait until the next service or sermon to hear the preacher, teacher, or leaders of the church speak before you are fed by the Word of God. You have the same opportunity as anyone else to read from the Bible and to gain downloads from the Holy Spirit. I am not saying you should not have a pastor. Yes, be connected to a church that has a sound doctrine and teachings that challenge you to become better. However, you should study the Word for yourself and be diligent and disciplined while making it a part of your life.

When I minister or counsel someone, it does not matter who they are. As soon as they begin to speak, I am able to detect if they have spent time with God. When you spend time with God, there is a different type of aura you give off, even when you are enduring a pressure point in your life. You must spend time with God. He will cleanse you. He will bring wholeness to your life. He will reveal it to you, and He will comfort you when you need it. At least to some extent, I see too many people who have been Christians for decades and are still being fed by the preacher. It is unacceptable. You must feed yourself. You have been in an immature state for too long.

The Ability to Speak the Truth in Love

Paul says you must speak the truth in love and grow in Christ (Ephesians 4:15–16). When you do this, the entire body grows in love. This is God's truth. This does not mean "keeping it real" or "keeping it 100." As many people say, "I am just telling the truth." This is still their opinion. When a person speaks God's truth, it must be done in love, and you must allow the Holy Spirit to guide you when you are speaking a truth. It should come from God, not from your own personal opinions and feelings. Too many people are speaking their feelings aloud, and it is causing harm to those they are speaking to. That is not the love God speaks about.

When you speak in godly love, the Holy Spirit will give you guidance in understanding how to deliver the message to someone. I hear too many people say they are just keeping it real. Guess what? That is your opinion of someone. It has nothing to do with the love of God. When you are able to speak in truth, with love, and allow the Holy Spirit to guide you through what has been downloaded in your mind, you can give the message to others. It will be without offense. They may not like it, but they will not be offended because it will line up with something they already know about themselves. As you continue to grow spiritually in Christ, you will have difficult conversations with believers. However, it should be in love, in grace, and in humility so that it pleases God.

When you begin to grow in grace, you must be willing to share the heart of God. You must not have a desire to harm those who have done you wrong. You should have a desire for your life to exist by the grace of God. You should not be in defense mode or respond with anger or revenge. When you have grown into maturity, you are able to respond from a place of forgiveness and grace.

When you begin to mature in God, you desire to be obedient to His Word. You want Him to be pleased with everything you do. The Bible tells you that if you love Christ, you will keep His commandments. That can be found in John 14:15. To please God, you must be faithful and obedient to His commands. Not out of obligation, but because you love Him. You do it out of gratitude for what Christ has done for you, and you do not take His agape love for granted.

In every stage of maturity in a person's life, from a newborn baby to an adult, what they eat changes as they mature. It is the same with those who are babies in Christ. As a newborn baby, you started off with milk and only drank liquids. This is the basic truth about God and His mighty acts and wondrous works. There is the expectation that you grow in your faith, in your understanding of Who He is. As you walk out the promises of God, at some point in the process of maturing, you must be able to chew by yourself. The pastor gives you the foundation to grow, and you have a responsibility to mature in every feeding until you can chew on your own. You are to be teachers of God's Word, but you must first grow and get an understanding of Who God is.

Let me be clear: Teaching God's Word does not mean you have to stand on a platform, or lecture at a podium or preach in the church. We are all called to discipleship and understand the Word of the Lord. However, when you reach the place of maturity, you have the ability to understand God's Word and execute the meaning of His Word through teaching others. Teaching the Word of God is an expectation of all Christians. I am not speaking of the gift of teaching, but the ability to translate and share with others about Christ, which is the responsibility of all Christians. I am speaking of discipleship. Matthew 28:19–20 says, "Go therefore and make disciples of all nations, baptizing them in the name of the Father and of the Son and of the Holy Spirit, teaching them to observe all things I have commanded you. And remember, I am with you always, even to the end of the age. Amen."

Galatians 5:23 gives you insight into the fruits of the spirit: love, joy, peace, patience, kindness, goodness, faithfulness, gentleness, self-control. A great way to determine whether you are growing is by evaluating the fruit in your life. Although you are all different, the fruit in your life should be visible to the people who see you, not just your own individual self-assessment.

You Are Involved in Community Engagement

We live in an environment where people are moving further away from the involvement of regular churches. However, the Bible explains that mature Christians should constantly and consistently meet together in a unified way. God created you for community. You must be intentional in the things you do concerning Christ. The writer of Hebrews encourages you to meet and come together in unity. When you have a love for Jesus Christ, it should cause you to desire to grow your understanding of Who He is so you can be more like Him and so the image of who you are looks like Him.

These were just a few tips on knowing when you are in a place of spiritual growth in your life.

You must forgive others, so God will forgive you. Matthew 6:14–15 tells us, "For if you forgive other people when they sin against you, your heavenly Father will also forgive you. But if you do not forgive others' sins, your Father will not forgive your sins."

1. Unite in church fellowship. You are taught in Proverbs 12:20, "Wise men walk in wise counsel."
2. You must pray to grow and connect with God. Remember, building an intimate relationship with God is imperative.
3. You should work to become a student of the Word and apply it to your life. God is the Word.

4. You must be humble. You must resist pride. God gives grace to those who are humble. In order to develop in Christ, you have to be teachable and humble.

At this point in the chapter, you should have grasped that spiritual growth increases your capability to deal with life challenges. It gives you the endurance and the ability to snap back when difficult situations come. Spiritual growth enhances your ability to deal with life's ups and downs and bounce back from those difficult experiences. It is easy to look at others with judgment and criticism, but when you start to grow spiritually, you realize how much healthier it is to cultivate and have sympathy for others. As you continue to grow and understand Who God is, your faith will begin to strengthen. What you desire for yourself begins to with the will of God.

Chapter Summary/Key Takeaways

As believers, you must grow spiritually so you can be effective in your God-given purpose. You, as a part of the church, have been given the power by God to shift the atmosphere and the trajectory of your situation. In order to do this, you must have a solid foundation rooted in the Word of God, so when the storm comes, you may bend, you may be tossed, but you will not break because you stand on the Word of God, the true and living Word. Prepare, because what you have learned spiritually will be needed as you continue on birthing your promise.

1. Become a student of the Word. Study to show yourself approved by God, a workman who needs not be ashamed, rightly dividing the word of truth (2 Timothy 2:15).
2. You are never too young or old to discover your purpose and help others.
3. It is easy to look at others with judgment and criticism, but when you start to grow spiritually, you realize how much healthier it is to cultivate and have sympathy for others.

The next chapter will provide an overview of why there is pain, suffering, and travail. It is not an easy process. However, there is a reason for God to stretch you to your capacity. The process is not easy, but it is necessary. We have to take into account that the process always comes before the promise. Prepare yourself, for the birth is soon to come.

CHAPTER 9

SPIRITUAL LABOR PAINS

But after you have suffered a little while, the
God of all grace, who has called us to His
eternal glory through Christ Jesus, will restore,
support, strengthen, and establish you.
—1 Peter 5:10

I want to reiterate that we must have a solid foundation rooted in the Word of God. This was discussed in the last chapter. Building a solid foundation ensures that when the storm comes, you do not break, you do not give up, you do not lose sight, and even if you bend, you will still stand on the true and living Word of God. When you can stand on God's Word, you are prepared to deal with the obstacles, hurdles, and turbulence that comes along with seeking the promise. Remember, the process must come before the promise. So, after you have gone through the storms and overcome the challenges, God will replenish, restore, rejuvenate, and establish you. Do not give up.

When women carry the promise of a baby in their womb, they are excited and full of joy. They are not just excited because they imagine the face of their unborn child. Rather, they understand that life is growing inside them, and at the appointed time, their child will be born, the seed God planted inside them, and their promise will come forth. The Father's promises to us as His children can be viewed in the same way. As you pursue your purpose, the only thing you have to go off of is God's promises.

Until we birth our purpose, all we have is the anticipation and the expectation that God's Word will do exactly what it says it will do, and that is, once we are obedient to the assignment that God has given us, we shall receive the promises of God. We have not yet seen the promises because we have not yet tapped into who and why we are; we have not begun walking in who God called us to be. You must identify, activate, and move forward with your purpose. Being a mother myself, I can assure you that when you carry a baby (or your purpose) in your womb, there will come a time and day when the birthing will take place. However, between the joy of giving birth and the promise, there is a stage before the birth that you must go through, and that is the travail, or labor. When the labor pains come, this is the time to make sure you have the overnight bag you prepared, call the list and your point person, and head to the hospital.

Remember, the delivery room is multifaceted and acts as the labor room, the birthing room, and the recovery room. Think of it as the trinity: "Father, Son, and Holy Spirit." It is indeed one. Therefore, you have come to the stage right before you birth your promise. Make sure you connect with your support system and the midwives because they will be needed during this time.

You are getting closer to your delivery date. However, your time to birth the promise has not yet come. You feel the pressure of the labor contractions, which signals to you that you are about to go into labor and birth the promise of God. Be careful. There is the possibility that you are experiencing false labor contractions. False labor makes you believe you are ready to give birth.

> The process always comes
> before the promise!
> ~ unknown

False Labor

This is why you must ensure you are connected to the right people. Because you are now anticipating the fulfillment of the promise, you must be cautious about who you allow to speak into you. You must understand that at this stage, you have to be able to separate the connections from God and those who are sent by the enemy. Be mindful and ensure that you ask God for wisdom, continue to seek His Word, and stay in prayer so you hear what the Holy Spirit says to you. You must protect the gift at all costs. Do not be fooled by the pressure you endured.

We must be able to determine the levels of pressure and where it is coming from because the enemy sends the pressures of detraction that make us feel like we cannot succeed. He tries to make us turn back from the promises of God. However, the pressure of God is extreme pressure that you experience to prepare you to carry out His plan. You must be able to identify the difference because if you are not careful, the deception of the enemy will cause you to deliver your gift prematurely. Many times, when a mother gives birth to a premature baby, there are complications that come along with it. There is the potential for chronic issues, and many times the baby has to stay in the hospital for a great length of time.

It is important that you are able to tell the difference between when the pressure is from the Holy Spirit and when the pressure is from the enemy. You must use wisdom and discernment to ensure you do not fall for the enemy's tactics and risk the promise. When you are experiencing a true contraction, it feels different from false labor pains because the pressure is more extreme. There is a discomfort and a pressure that is almost unbearable. When you have true contractions, the pressure of the contractions come closer together as time passes. However, false labor contractions do not get closer together and can be irregular.

Once you understand the difference between false labor and true labor pains, you can prevent the risk of moving before God has released you for the chosen time. As you endure the pressures of false labor, you realize God still has some stretching for you to do in your life, even through the pressure. Stay the course, because the pressure will become more extreme as God stretches you to birth the promise. Do not lose sight of the promise. There is still some stretching that must take place in order for you to birth what God has put in you. He stretched you according to the size of what you carried.

Real Labor Pains

When you begin to experience intense or severe pain, you have entered into the final stage of birthing your purpose. You are one step closer to seeing the manifestation of what God has promised. At this point, you may feel as though you cannot take any more. 1 Corinthians 10:13 says, "No temptation has taken you except what is common to man. God is faithful, and He will not permit you to be tempted beyond what you can endure but will with the temptation also make a way to escape, that you may be able to bear it."

God will never give you more than you can handle or withstand. You are being pruned at this point. You are stronger than you think. God knows. He allows pressure because He knows you can handle it. When you are trying to give birth to what God has put inside you, your mind tells you that you cannot make it, that you should give up, that you are a failure, and that you will never see the manifestation of God's promise in your life. I come to tell you, that is a lie. Continue to endure, even when you are pushed to the limits and extremities of your confidence and faith in the Father. Hold on to God's Word and put your trust in Him. You must not give up. The journey you are on is ordained by God. It is the very reason He created you. You must not give up. Keep the faith as you endure; there is always a time in the process when you must be strong. Hold fast because you are in the stages of labor that prepare you for delivery. You will be uncomfortable because your faith will be tested, and it will be stretched beyond what you believe to be your capacity.

Although the Holy Spirit and the Word of God are your first level of support, God sends a support team that has been preordained to help you through every aspect of labor and delivery. They will speak affirmations, pray, and intercede, and they will confess the prophecy of God until they see the manifestation of what God promised come forth. They declare the Word of the Lord, assist in carrying you through the process, and speak downloads from the Holy Spirit with accuracy. This is a part of their God-given assignment. Chapter 7 provides you with more information on your support team, including the midwives.

There were many times throughout the Bible when people's faith was tested during the journey that was attached to their assignment from God.

Abraham stretched out his arm to sacrifice his son, Isaac. Abraham had faith in God. He believed that whatever God promised him would come to pass; therefore, he was willing to sacrifice his son. David was running for his life because Saul and his enemies wanted him dead. And Joseph had to endure disloyalty, captivity, and adversity before he finally understood the realization of his dream. The same is true for our lives. If we endure and stay focused until completion, we will inherit the promise of God. We should stand firm on this because His words never return void. "We must not grow weary in doing good, for in due season, we shall reap, if we do not give up" (Galatians 6:9).

The Water Breaks

When a woman is close to delivering her baby, there is a point during the process where her water breaks. This signifies that labor has begun. After her water breaks, the mother-to-be should contact her doctor and head to the hospital. The water breaks when the baby is ready to make his or her entrance into the world. Once your water breaks, you can expect the birth to take place soon. You must stay focused and strong during the process. It is critical and vital for the birth to come forth. Remember, we talked about your gifts lying dormant inside of you in Chapter 3. There has to be an awakening and a discovery in the beginning stages of the process. Now it is time to give birth to the promise.

Once you make it through the process, you realize doors are going to open to fulfill the plan of God. Even though the process has been long and the pain has been excruciating, you will soon give birth to your destiny. It is time to come out of hibernation. It is time to come out of the darkness, out of those former places and what used to be. "Therefore, if any man is in Christ, he is a new creature. Old things have passed away. Look, all things have become new" (2 Corinthians 5:17). It is time for you to walk in your newness, to be confident in who you are in Christ, and to stand firm on His Word. It is your time to be released into the very thing God has created you for.

As you walk in your newness, you must continue to carry the fact that God favors you. You were conceived by the Holy Spirit. The seed of purpose that was planted inside you will come forth so the spirit of God that is functioning inside you can be renewed, restored, revived, redeveloped, reinforced, rejuvenated, restarted, and rekindled. Prepare. Because the birthing season is upon you. Remember when Mary asked the angel Gabriel why God chose her to carry the Messiah, Jesus Christ? Gabriel told Mary that God highly favored her. It is the same for you. God favors you. He loves you with an agape love. He created you to carry out His plans on Earth.

I shared before how valuable the gift is and that it is growing inside of you. We talked about how the Holy Spirit supernaturally impregnated Mary. Just as Mary carried the Messiah, Jesus Christ, you carry a promise that will shift the atmosphere and change the trajectory as long as you submit and are obedient to the assignments of God. We also discussed Elizabeth, Mary's cousin, who gave birth to John the Baptist, the prophet whose assignment was to announce the coming of the Messiah. God will put people in your path on purpose, and you will be required to support them because they will be carrying the promise of God and are attached to the call. You will be their support system. What do I mean? There will be people God places in your path who carry the same gift as you. God will enable you to work in harmony with others, without discord and conflict.

The time will come when you must be prepared. There will be many people who have the same gift. You must understand that there is room in this world for every gift to be utilized. We are all unique in the execution of how we function in our gifts. You cannot see someone else's gift as a threat. You have to use your gift to help others be in pursuit of theirs.

Even when times feel difficult, God is doing a new work in you. He does not care how difficult it feels for you. Every assignment he gives you, he equips you to complete it in accordance with His desire and will. He must get the glory. There will be times you are uncomfortable, just as you are in this stage of travail. However, you must understand that your uncomfortable place is where you grow and learn, but more importantly, it is necessary and will be required by God to bring you into the purpose and plan He prophesied over your life. Do not give up. No matter how uncomfortable it gets, do not give up and do not quit, for the reward is soon to come.

Have you ever worked a job and given two weeks' notice? As the time gets closer to the end, you can feel the pressure, the tenseness, and the anxiety of every aspect of that role you are waiting to be released from. When everything is said and done, those two weeks feel like two months. From the time you put in your notice until the two weeks are up, you are ready to walk out because you have had enough. Everything irritates you because you know that a new job is waiting for you. However, you understand that if you just walk out, there may be consequences in the future if you need a job recommendation. Your character would not let you do it.

It is the same with our walk with Christ as we continue to wait for the birth of what we carry. The discomfort only intensifies. We must make sure we are not anxious. Philippians 4:6–7 says, "We should be anxious about nothing, but in everything, by prayer and supplication with gratitude, make your requests known to God." And the peace of God, which surpasses all understanding, will protect your hearts and minds through Christ Jesus. Be careful about inducing labor to fulfill the promise before time. Accept the plan of God and the time He has appointed for the birth to take place. We were all born at an appointed time. The Word of God says, "God knew of us before the wombs of our mothers." He knew us and set us apart, meaning He made us unique and according to His plan. God called you forth when he spoke your name! which means He knew your name before your parents chose it for you.

Once the mother-to-be arrives at the hospital, is admitted into the labor and delivery room, and begins to have contractions or labor pains, the nurses come in to prepare and position her so she can deliver the baby. My suggestion to you is to hold on a little longer and do not faint or back down. You must get into a position to birth the promise you have been carrying. John 16:21 says, "When a woman is giving birth, she has pain because her hour has come. But as soon as she delivers the child, she no longer remembers the anguish for the joy that a child is born into the world."

The Pressure of Travail

As the pressure intensifies, you must be able to identify the pressures that come from God. You face many pressures. You face pressure from the world and pressure from the Holy Spirit to help condition you for the assignment God has given you. Make sure when you are under pressure that you stay prayerful and continue to build a relationship with Christ through the reading of His Word. You cannot afford to give up or lay your life on the line and allow the enemy to cause you to abort the promise at this stage. You have come too far to turn around or to shift back to an old mindset. You must own your newness.

Make sure you continue to stay connected to the Holy Spirit so you receive guidance on the things of God. The Holy Spirit will give you instructions on what you should do to ensure you are in the will of God. You must resist the devil using the word of truth, and I can assure you that he will flee. As you continue to fight through the pressures of life, you will continue to gain strength and endurance for situations that may come your way. After you have suffered a little while, the God of all grace, who has called us to His eternal glory through Christ Jesus, will restore, support, strengthen, and establish you. Keep in mind that it is under extreme pressure that diamonds are created. Hang in there, and do not give up. God wants to reveal the diamond in you.

The Stretching

You are in the final stages of the process. You have gone through the false labor and pushed on, identifying the enemy's pressures and distractions. You have made it through the breaking and the heaviness, and you are in the place of dilatation. You will feel the pressure of God stretching you. When a woman gives birth to a baby, her body has to dilate to a certain dimension before the baby can be born. When you are in the process of birthing the promise of God, all the things you endure during this time are transitions, positioning, and stretching so you have the character, the identity, and the strength to fulfill the plan of God once the birthing happens. God wants you to be prepared for spiritual maturity.

According to God's plan, at this point, you should be able to share the good news of Christ.

Transitioning from what you have always done to being stretched and growing in the things of God is not always fun. The process can be uncomfortable and awkward at times. There are times in your life when God develops and stretches you, making you uncomfortable. I am here to tell you to stay the course in the uncomfortable, because when things get uncomfortable, you recognize that a shift is about to come. God has to stretch you according to the size of your purpose. He has to ensure that during the pushing process you have stretched wide enough for your purpose to pass through the various obstacles and boundaries that may arise.

Remember, I said you are highly favored. Therefore, when you get to an uncomfortable place, know that this occurs right before God gives you a breakthrough. Seeking Christ and the Holy Spirit will enhance how you think, improve your behavior, and determine how you respond during times of discomfort. Continuously seeking Him, hungry and thirsty after the Father, will cause you to understand what love truly is. You will desire to walk in love, speak in love, and fulfill the plan of God in love, because God is love. It is important to be a student of the Word of God because His Word will satisfy your thirst, which causes you to desire Him even more.

In Position and Posture to Birth the Promise

The promise is upon you. Do not fear the transition that is about to take place. There will be a shift now because the time for the birth has come. I warn you to embrace what the Lord is about to do in your life. Time is of the essence. You have been waiting for this day to come. God is going to add to you in this season and not subtract anything. You will not lose, because the plan of God does not include subtraction. You may have felt as though the pressures of life have been unbearable and you could not complete the process. However, I prophesy that God is about to cause you to expand from the east to the west, to the north and the south. 1 Chronicle 4:10 says, "Jabez called on the God of Israel, saying, 'Oh, that you would indeed bless me and enlarge my territory, that your hand might be with me, and that you would keep *me* from evil, that *it* may not bring me hardship!' So, God granted what he asked." God will grant you an expansion far beyond your current territory because you have His favor and protection over your life." This time is soon to come. If you stay on course with the things of God and are obedient to the God-given assignments, He will begin to trust you. He will begin to open doors that you never thought you would walk through.

When you walk in obedience, God will begin to trust you. He will add to your life when you truly transform your mindset to think like Christ. You must get rid of the old person and put on the new man. The Word of the Lord proclaims that "whoever can be trusted with very little can also be trusted with much, and whoever is dishonest with very little will also be dishonest with much" (Luke 16:10). You are now in your birthing season. Do not be surprised that when you are in the birthing season, it can be an unpleasant and difficult transition. However, once a mother goes through labor, endures the pain, and pressures that come with it, once she has given birth, the pain no longer exists. Prepare yourself for childbirth because God is about to pour into you. You are in your final stretch. Do not give up. You are worthy. You are more than enough, and you are worth every promise and prophecy God has ordained and spoken over your life. Prepare, because the appointed time has come.

Chapter Summary/Key Takeaways

The pressure of travail is not easy. You cannot afford to give up. Remember, God will add to your life when you truly transform your mindset to think like Christ. When you walk in obedience, you learn more and more about God. Listen to the Holy Spirit so you may hear what the Lord is saying during the time of travail.

1. The pressure of your pain builds endurance to withstand the stretching that is required to birth the purpose you carry.
2. God wants you to mature in Him. Spiritual development improves your ability to deal with life's ups, downs and recover from adversity.

The next chapter is about giving birth to your promise. When God stretches you to His capacity, you must ensure you are prepared for delivery. God stretches past what you think are your boundaries and causes growth spurts along the way. When the appointed time comes, you will know because the pain and pressure of travail are unbearable. The birthing season is upon you.

CHAPTER 10

————————◆————————

BIRTHING YOUR PURPOSE

Trust in the Lord with all your heart and lean
not on your own understanding; in all your ways
acknowledge Him, and He will direct your paths.
—Proverbs 3:5–6

We must remember that labor and birth lead to the promise of God. I thank God that "He is not a man, that He should lie, nor a son of man, that He should repent. Has He spoken, and will He not do it? Or has He spoken, and will He not make it good?" (Numbers 23:19). When God promises something, He will bring it to pass. God will never bring us to a moment where we give birth and not deliver. God is not a man who would lie. And the fact that you are struggling, fighting, and laboring for it is the undisputable and unquestionable reality that it already exists. When a woman is pregnant with a baby, the fact of the matter is that the baby already exists in her womb. It is no different when it comes to the promise of God.

God's promise is not something you are trying to develop or speak into existence. The reality is that it already exists. Even in its dormant stage, it exists. It is there. However, there must be an awakening or activation so it begins to grow. When you labor over the promise of God, you are in travail over a thing or a promise, and that is

> You can no longer live like
> you are in the incubating season.
> That season has passed! You are
> no longer incubating the seed
> ~ Daphne Jett

115

evident. The promise already exists inside you; it is growing inside of you. Whatever has been birthed in you has been imparted into you through the Holy Spirit, the Word of God, or a prophetic word. If the impartation comes from God, He promises that it will come forth. He will bring it to pass. "Truly I have spoken; truly I will bring it to pass." When you are in the process of conception, labor, or travail and delivery, you must be mindful of what you say out of your mouth by putting on a new mind and speaking in a Christlike manner.

To travail means to labor, endure pain, bear, bring forth, and be anxious. I can relate to many of these symptoms when I was at a place of prayer and trusting God, squeezing the last of my faith that God would bring forth the promises that He planned for my life. It was not easy to endure. During the unbearable times in your life, when there is extreme pressure, suffering, stretching, and travail, God has promised He will deliver that which He placed inside you. He has promised that the birth will occur at the appointed time. God will always keep His promises. He has never made a promise that He has not kept. If God said it, you can count on it coming to pass. His Word will do exactly what He sent it to do. His Word will not be rendered ineffective. This is just a benefit of caring about your purpose.

Delivering the promise is the gift. Psalm 127:3 says, "Look, children are a gift from the Lord, and the fruit of the womb is a reward." Continue to have faith and press through the stretching, travail, and pushing. You will see the greatness of God if you do not faint. Do not let go of the promise. Never give up. Stay the course. God's greatness already exists on earth, and it will come forth and manifest in the delivery room.

In Genesis 3:16, God reveals that it was not until Abraham and Eve were disobedient and ate from the tree of life that He punished Eve by multiplying her pain in childbirth; she would experience pain when she gave birth to her babies. You must realize that you are going to have to go through being stretched, enduring the pressure, and being uncomfortable at every step of the process. God is building endurance, strength, character, identity, and power so you are prepared to birth the promise and so you have everything you need to go forth and speak into the lives of His sons and daughters, fulfilling His plan on earth. So, as you go through this process, if you feel as though you are at the breaking point, do not pray for God to take the experience from you because of the travail and the pain.

Continue to tolerate and be brave because the Word of the Lord says that "a man's gift makes room for him, and brings him before great men" (Proverbs 18:16). God takes us through the suffering and travail; before He clears the way for us to go before great men, He prepares and equips us. It does not matter how tired you get, how exhausted you are from being pregnant with the promise of God, do not get weary as you go through this process. When a woman is pregnant with a baby, the pregnancy is divided into three stages, or trimesters. At this point, you are in your third trimester and ready to deliver. This is not the time to abort the promise; this is the time to "pray without ceasing" (1 Thessalonians 5:17), because the time has come that you must prepare to push.

Prepare to Push

When you get to the place of birthing the promise of God, this is the stage where God begins to position you for the delivery. Once you have been stretched, there is no more capacity for you to stretch further. The appointed time is upon you, and now that God has positioned you, it is time for you to deliver. It is important to prepare for the push before you begin to push! Be careful not to push too soon. Pushing when you are not ready can cause you to prematurely give birth to your purpose without finishing out the process. Also, when you begin to push, you will experience an increase in pressure. Once it is time to push, you will feel a strong natural urge to bear down and throw in the towel. Do not give up! You are too close! Going through the birthing process helps you truly take hold of the power of prayer and understand the impact. I remember being in the delivery room, and when it was time for me to have my son, the pain and the pressure I endured caused me to pray to the Father that I would make it through the experience of birthing life into the earth. During my birthing season, I realized that although my suffering and travail may have included pain, it was also equipped with God's purpose.

I thought about Job, who suffered for a long time. However, in our suffering, there is also God's purpose. Job was one example in the Bible that helped me recognize that in our suffering, there is pain. Job 1:1 explains that God advised Satan to have a high regard for Job because he was "blameless, righteous, and honorable." And after God allowed the devil to afflict Job with agonizing and excruciating sores, God wanted the devil to recognize Job's commitment to Christ while he was suffering. Here we have the Father, Who is having a conversation with Satan, and Satan has to get permission from God before causing affliction on Job. He has to state his case about causing affliction to God's sons and daughters, and he cannot cause pain, suffering, or distress until he gets approval from the Father. There are too many people in life suffering because they do not believe God allows us to go through suffering.

I have heard many people ask, "Why would God allow us to go through suffering, especially if we have been faithful?" Christ suffered a lot. He suffered on His way to the cross. We are talking about the Son of God, who is perfect in all His ways and who suffered not because of His own sins but for the sins of the world. Forgiveness of our sins was willingly paid for by Christ. Jesus had to endure the pain so we could be forgiven and have eternal life. This was God's purpose and plan behind Christ's pain.

We can inspect every area in our lives and identify with any type of pain or suffering, but we must understand that God's purpose has been planted in us; it proclaims His expressed assurance that you have the strength to tolerate the burdens He allows you to go through. You have gone through stretching, you have gone through the pain and suffering, but as you enter the delivery room, the extremities of your pain will become unbearable. Stay focused because once the birthing happens, the process of your pain and suffering will not be remembered. The Bible proclaims, "When a woman is giving birth, she has pain, because her hour has come. But as soon as she delivers the child, she no longer remembers the anguish and rejoices that a child has been born into the world" (John 16:21).

"We know that the whole creation has been groaning as in the pains of childbirth right up to the present time" (Romans 8:22). The birthing season is upon you. The journey and process have been nothing more than a time of labor and delivery pains. Throughout this process, there have been so many different trials, circumstances, and painful things that have happened to try to take me off course and distract me in hopes that I will abort the promise. For me, in my experience of becoming a mother in the natural and birthing the God-given gift from within, it has been like child birthing pains that continued to intensify as I got closer to labor and delivery. Do you realize that your promise awaits you? Have you yet to see your best days? No, the best of your life is ahead of you. God is birthing something in your life that is bigger than you can even think or imagine. It is time for you to push, push, push. I know there is extreme pressure, but your final push has come. Be ready to position yourself for the abundant life that God speaks about in John 10:10, "I came that they may have life, and that they may have it more abundantly."

Time to Give Birth to the Promise

Our God has stretched you beyond what you thought were your limits; it is the stretching that leads you to believe you cannot handle the pressure or go any further, but our God will never leave you or forsake you. Stretching is never a comfortable spot to be in, nor an easy process to withstand. However, if you are comfortable, you are not learning. It is in your uncomfortable places that God stretches past what you believe to be your boundaries and causes growth spiritually along the way (Proverbs 24:10). If you faint in the face of adversity, your strength is small. God will stay with you as you go through the process.

God has stretched you past the boundaries of your limitations and abilities so you can be launched into His promise. Isaiah 40:29–31 says, "He gives power to the faint, and to those that have no might, he increases strength." We all grow weary, we all stumble and fall short of the glory of God, whether we are young or old. However, we must have faith that God will renew our strength. We all have a desire to receive the blessings and promises of God. Many of us pray and ask God to show us favor; we desire the promises and blessings of God. However, we have to realize that carrying the promise of God means there will be some stretching and suffering, and you will be inconvenienced until the promise comes forth. You must be patient and not give up until God's appointed time to call forth the promise. Remember that the promise of God is not about you. Now that you have birthed the gift, you have a responsibility to obey, to listen, and to respond to the assignment God has given you. You are responsible for the lives that are attached to your gift.

"That which is born of the flesh is flesh, and that which is born of the spirit is spirit" (John 3:6). Therefore, humans can reproduce human life, but it is the Holy Spirit Who gives birth to spiritual life. God has brought forth your gift, which is the reason you exist. It is the very reason He breathed the breath of life into you. God has given you the gift; therefore, He accepts the gift. Nothing is too big or too small when God accepts it. One of the things I realized as I went through the process of birthing what God put inside me was that there was a responsibility not to man but to God, that I would align with the gift. This means that as you move forward and begin to nurture your gift, you use it for the glory of God, that He may get the glory out of every situation and assignment that He gives you.

The Bible tells us that too much is given and too much is required (Luke 12:48). God holds us responsible for what He has given us. We are supposed to utilize our gift to benefit the lives of others. When we serve the Lord using our gifts, we bring glory to the name of God. However, we also bring blessings to His sons and daughters. This pleases God. It pleases God because it fulfills His plan. God will hold you accountable to His expectations, even more so now that the promise has been fulfilled. Use your gifts to serve others and continue to be in alignment with the things of God and model a servant's heart.

You must have the mindset and the desire to serve others. It does not matter how you feel towards them or how much it may cost you. The Holy Spirit will guide you into a place of walking in the will of the Father, so you must exercise your gift of serving others.

I was recently telling a dear friend about the call on her life. I told her she could not afford to resist the gift God gave her. She knew she must make full use of the gift and the calling that had been revealed in her life, because if she did not utilize what God had given her, other people would pay the price for not receiving from her the gift that was given to her to bless others. As 1 Peter 4:10 reminds us that "as everyone has received a gift, even so serve one another with it, as good stewards of the manifold grace of God." If she refused to utilize the gift God gave her, she would have to give account to God. We will all have to give an account of ourselves to God. Romans 14:12 says, "So then each of us shall give an account of himself to God." At that moment, I told her now was not the time to make excuses for not doing the right thing at the right moment. I read this quote by Habeeb Akande, a British-Nigerian writer, who said, "The lazier a man is, the more he plans to do tomorrow." We have to move in obedience to God. God wants our yes. Using your God-given gifts matters. After all the hell you have endured through the birthing process, why wouldn't you want to use the gift God has given you?

The Release

With a new mindset, new thoughts, a new way of doing things, and a shift in how you respond to the assignments of God and the birthing of purpose, you must continue in prayer, reading the Word, fasting, worshiping, and repenting as you give out to others. You must walk in your calling with the expectation that the lives you are assigned to will draw near to God as you impart and impact their lives with God's Word. It is time to walk and fulfill all that God has prophesied for your life.

You can no longer live like you are in the incubating season. That season has passed. You are no longer incubating the seed. The expectation God has for you is of a higher calling. Every hindrance, every sound, every distraction, every struggle, every insecurity, every addiction, everything that prevents you or blocks you from advancing in the Kingdom in alignment with the call on your life has to be removed in the name of Jesus. These things can no longer be found in your dwelling; "you have been called to greater, you have been destined for more." Therefore, you have to relinquish anything and everything that does not align you with the will of God.

As you continue on this journey of fulfilling your God-given call, the Lord will release new assignments. You must be open to new assignments that make you uncomfortable. It is important to be flexible in the assignments and tasks God gives you. He will give you priorities, and you must take on these assignments from heaven and be flexible to move with effectiveness and stay focused on your stage in Christ. When we realize what our gifts accomplish and achieve for the family of God and accept the fact that we are not all the same, we increase and carry God's love to more than one place, which intensifies and deepens the impact we have on the lives of the Lord's sons and daughters within our realm of influence.

God knows the people who will be drawn to His heart through the gifts, abilities, and resources each of us has. It is not enough to just discover the gift and birth it; we must embrace it and use our gift to bring Christ to the light through walking in love and touching the lives of others; this fulfills God's plan on earth. It is the power of Jesus that gives us the freedom to practice our gifts and to grow to our fullest potential in them. Deuteronomy 8:18 reminds us that "we must remember the Lord your God, for it is He who gives you the ability to get wealth, so that He may establish His covenant which He swore to your fathers, as it is today."

So, because of Who Jesus is, and because He died on the cross for us, we now have the freedom to serve God and people with the gifts that come from Him. We should not withhold our gifts from others. 1 Corinthians 12:27–28 says, "Now you are the body of Christ and members individually. God has put these in the church: first apostles, second prophets, third teachers, after that miracle, then gifts of healing, help, government, and various tongues." We must use our gift to impact lives and change hearts in the hope that we draw people near to God, according to His plan. Colossians 3:17 says, "And whatever you do in word or deed, do all in the name of the Lord Jesus, giving thanks to God the Father through Him." So, as we serve God through our calling and purpose, we bring honor to Him. Taking the honor and glory from God is a form of robbing Him because that glory was never for us; it has always been for Him.

Chapter Summary/Key Takeaways

The day and hour have finally arrived. You have completed the process. That which was given to you and divinely mandated before time began has come to pass. The seed God placed in you has matured and is ready to be used by the Master. It is time to emerge from the shadows! Come out of the shadows, and let God utilize you mightily. The church has been anticipating what God has invested in you. It is important that you move with a servant's heart! And a willingness to do God's will. The appointed time has arrived. This is a purposeful process. The pressure of your pain builds endurance to withstand the stretching that is required to birth the purpose you carry.

1. It is time to come out of hiding and move forward in your God-given purpose.
2. Allow God to use you mightily by coming out of darkness and into the light.
3. The church has been looking forward to God's investment in you.

Never stop pursuing God. He loves you and desires you to love Him. Continue to keep your support system as you perfect and protect the gift because it has value. The lives of others are hanging in the balance of your decision to move forward. Remember, do not give up, no matter who you are. God still wants to use you. Birthing the gift that God has placed within you will fill voids in your life that you will never be able to fill on your own.

Prayer To Find Purpose

Father God, thank you for creating me with a divine purpose. Father, please forgive me of every sin that has separated me from your purpose for my life, in Jesus' name. In the name of Jesus, show me the purpose I have to fulfill. Lord, help me to identify and embrace your purpose for my life in the name of Jesus. Please open my eyes to see the purpose that you have for my life. Let that purpose that you have for me be revealed in the name of Jesus. As I establish intimacy with you, Lord, reveal my true identity to you. That I can get to know myself without the constraints of the outside world's perspectives and perceptions. In the name of Jesus, I refuse to work against the purpose of God for my life. Lord, I ask that you order my steps so that as I am in pursuit of my purpose, I want to help others and fulfill your plan on earth. Lord, I desire to be more like you. Please open my eyes so that I can see clearly as I move forward in my journey. Lord, awaken my purpose and connect me with people that see in me what you see in me, father. From this day forward, I will be in pursuit of my purpose. I will not give up! until the I birth my purpose.

ACKNOWLEDGMENTS

To **Evangelist Maxine L. "Aunt Pinky" Ross**, I express my gratitude for introducing me to Jesus Christ, our Lord and Savior. Your introduction provided me with an opportunity to hear from Him and walk in obedience by authoring this book.

To **Deaconess Eleanor Bowman, "Aunty,"** you are indeed an example of the light of God. Thank you for being a listening ear, providing God's agape love, and being consistent in your love for God and me. Thank you for your discipleship. You have set the bar high. I am so grateful for the opportunity to absorb the residue of who you are in Christ and allow it to be reflected in my writing of who He is.

To **Elder Michael and Minister Karen King**, you both have been an instrument in my life and the wings beneath my wings. Thank you for loving me through my pain, hurt, and pitfalls. I am grateful for your love and for never giving up on me. You both have guided and taught me about being strong in the Lord. Without your investment, I would not have been able to carry the weight of writing to completion.

To **Deaconess Kelly Armstrong**, my sister and friend, thank you for your time spent over the years, pushing me and prophesying God's Word over my life. Even when I did not understand it, you did. I am thankful for the spirit of God that rests in you and your consistent and authentic love. I thank God for every prophetic word you spoke over my life, down to God's expectations for me to author this book. It is finished.

To **Apostle Anita Dawson, "Lady Overflow,"** you have been a friend, a listener, and a supporter. I am forever grateful. Thank you for being there when I needed someone the most. I am thankful for your knowledge and mentorship. Every nugget of wisdom you shared with me has served as a foundation for my writing.

Reverend (Prophet) Deandra Jenkins, you taught me how to pray the Word of God in the good times and in the bad times, to delve deeper into His Word, and to intercede on His behalf. Thank you for your mentorship. I love you for life. Because of you, I understand the intimate place in God that I compose in this book. Through my writing and intimate times with Christ during this process, I am reminded of every word you have spoken to me.

To **Apostle David Carter** of the Worship Center of Central Ohio, thank you for imparting spiritual conception and transformation of the apostolic, inducing the prophetic gifting of spiritual contractions through the laying of hands. 1 Timothy 4:14 tells us that we should "not neglect your gift, which was given to you through prophecy when the body of elders laid their hands on you." Areas within this book were built on spiritual conception.

To **Pastor Richard "Rick" Jones**, the executive pastor of the City of Grace Church, Columbus, Ohio, for being a part of my support system. You identified with my gift and continued to prophesy it daily until it began to manifest. Because of the encouragement you gave me, I was inspired and empowered to write this book. I can remember shaking before speaking engagements, and you would go into hype man mode. Your encouragement is always a reminder of the power of God that rests in me.

To **Pastor Michael A. Young**, the shepherd of the City of Grace Church, Columbus, Ohio. What can I say? You are a trendsetter in the kingdom. You have been a mentor, pastor, cheerleader, supporter, and pusher of the gospel. Thank you for believing in the call on my life, for being obedient to God and calling me out of my comfortable place, for watering, investing, teaching, and sowing time into my gift. You walked me through every growing trimester concerning the call on my life. It is incredible how you forced me to push through my labor pains, stretching me to an uncomfortable place that positioned and prepared me for delivery. The pain, suffering, and pressure of it all were worth it. I am forever grateful to you for seeing in me what God sees. My experience at the City of Grace changed my life. It took me to a place of discovery. I wrote this book with every investment, every correction, every time spent, every word of encouragement, every nugget, and every story related to my life in the Bible. I drafted this book based on the push. You pushed me into some uncomfortable territory. I could not have written this book if you had not called me out of a place of no movement and into activating the call on my life. I am grateful to you. I love you for life. You have been an investor in my life.

To the TPAK family, *Prophet Hope Melton, Apostle Monique Jackson, Apostle Brian Carroll, Apostle Vertina Hunt.* Each of you has been the cord to my instrument. Without your display of leadership, teaching, authenticity, and encouragement, I would never have come out of hiding. Whew, I can breathe. You all have been leading me from your seats, and I am forever grateful to you. You each inspired me to go for it and to be confident in who God has called me to be and to embrace it. I salute each of you. Because of you, I was able to give life to this book.

To **Pastor Carmela Head**: Thank you to my literature coach, my sister in Christ. You are a true example of grace and virtue. Thank God for you and your time and commitment to reading my literature and for talking me off the ledge, providing feedback, and meeting with me weekly to keep me on track until the end. I could not have done this without you; I was able to write with expectancy because of you. Thank you for allowing me the opportunity to meet Daphne during this journey. You are unique, and I cannot wait to see all that God has for you. You are indeed a woman of grace and virtue. Thank you for visiting me at the finish line.

To **Apostle Patrick Brown**: Whew, what can I say? Thank you for pastoring, mentoring, teaching, and coaching me when I needed it most. I never thought our paths would cross again when I needed it most. God is strategic. You are the epitome of a phenomenal leader. I am so grateful for your apostolic and prophetic leadership, which has set me ablaze regarding the apostolic and prophetic. You challenge me to exceed the limits of what I believe to be my boundaries. You applied pressure until this book manifested. You charge me with the words that I spoke and challenge me to understand what it means to be obedient to God and what my yes looks like on every assignment from Him. You applied pressure throughout this process. Whew. You showed me what movement looks like. Thank you for holding me accountable for the responsibilities of my God-given purpose. This book is because of you. Without your continuous checkups, calls, and investing, I would not have made my assignment a reality. I love you for how my life has been changed through your leadership and mentorship. The Jett family loves you, sir.

The time has come for me to head to the delivery room, where the birth must take place.

REFERENCES

Brenner, Dan. "What to Know about Ultrasound to Learn Baby's Sex." WebMD. WebMD, June 15, 2021. https://www.webmd.com/baby/what-to-know-ultrasound-babys-sex

Burch, Kelly. "Conception: Timeline, Process, Signs, and Preparation." Verywell Health. www.verywellhealth.com, October 19, 2021. https://www.verywellhealth.com/conception-5115035.

Ciccarelli, David. "Start, Stop, Continue Tutorial." Forbes. www.forbes.com, February 2, 2016. https://www.forbes.com/sites/groupthink/2016/02/02/start-stop-continue-tutorial/?sh=2b72c11e2798.

Printed in the United States
by Baker & Taylor Publisher Services